Worker Participation and American Unions

Threat or Opportunity?

Thomas A. Kochan - Harry C. Katz
Nancy R. Mower

Massachusetts Institute of Technology

1984

The W. E. Upjohn Institute for Employment Research

Library of Congress Cataloging in Publication Data

Kochan, Thomas A.
   Worker participation and American unions.

   Bibliography: p.

   1. Industrial management—United States—Employee
participation.   2. Trade-unions—United States.   I. Katz,
Harry Charles, 1951-   II. Mower, Nancy R.
III. Title.
HD5660.U5K62   1984   658.3'152'0973   84-13071
ISBN 0-88099-021-X
ISBN 0-88099-022-8 (pbk.)

THE AUTHORS

Thomas A. Kochan and Harry C. Katz are faculty members and Nancy Mower is a research associate at the Industrial Relations Section, Sloan School of Management, Massachusetts Institute of Technology. This book grows out of a larger on-going research project involving the authors and their colleagues at the Industrial Relations Section titled "U.S. Industrial Relations in Transition."

Professor Kochan received his Ph.D. from the University of Wisconsin and was a member of the faculty of the New York State School of Industrial and Labor Relations, Cornell University, prior to coming to MIT in 1980. Professor Katz has been at MIT since receiving his Ph.D. from University of California, Berkeley in 1977. Ms. Mower received her MS in Management from MIT in 1982.

FOREWORD

In May of 1982, the Industrial Union Department's (IUD) Labor Policy Institute initiated a project to assess the impact on trade unions and collective bargaining of worker participation or quality of worklife plans.

Individual unions have had different experiences with, and reactions to, such programs. In some cases unions have rejected such plans, citing their negative impact on collective bargaining. In other situations, typically those involving unions that have been integrally involved in formulating and operating worker participation programs, the reaction has been much more positive. Given this diversity, we thought that it would be useful to sponsor research that could document the variety of positive and negative experiences unions have encountered.

Professor Tom Kochan from MIT, who undertook the research with his colleagues Harry Katz and Nancy Mower, has had wide experience in the field of industrial relations. In addition, a number of IUD affiliates assisted the MIT researchers in defining the questions and helped assess the results of the study. We owe special thanks to those unions which made special efforts to facilitate access to members and officials for Professor Kochan and his associates.

We feel that this study is a useful tool for workers considering participation in QWL and QWL-related schemes. Those contemplating such approaches will, as a result of this research, be better able to identify pitfalls as well as a variety of means for enhancing the potential success of their efforts.

Howard D. Samuel, *President*
Industrial Union Department, AFL-CIO

CONTENTS

Chapter 1

What's the Problem?

The growth of quality of working life (QWL) programs, related forms of worker participation processes, and experiments with new forms of work organization in the past decade have posed both new challenges and potential opportunities to the American labor movement. On the one hand, these informal mechanisms require union leaders and managers to modify their traditional roles and relationships in significant ways. On the other hand, they open new channels for direct worker involvement and, possibly, for greater worker and union influence. These developments have generated a vigorous debate among union leaders concerning whether QWL and related participation processes will, in the long run, be good or bad for labor unions and for the workers they represent. Yet, the debate has, to date, largely taken place in a vacuum. While strong rhetorical arguments have been presented by both the supporters and the critics of worker participation processes, little direct examination of union experiences with these processes has informed the discussions.

In early 1982, however, a group of labor leaders meeting under the auspices of the Industrial Union Department of the AFL-CIO agreed to commission an independent study of the experiences of unions with worker participation processes. The processes studied operate under a variety of

1

labels in addition to QWL, such as Quality Circles (QC), Employee Involvement (EI), Labor-Management Participation Teams (LMPT), socio-technical work systems, etc. The purpose of this book is to report the results of that study. The common characteristics of the QWL and related forms of worker participation studied are that all these programs involve small groups of union members and/or officers in informal workplace participation processes which supplement the formal collective bargaining procedures. Some of these programs also go on to modify the way jobs and work are structured and organized at the workplace. These shop floor or office level forms of *direct* worker participation stand in contrast to the more long-standing form of *indirect* participation commonly found in U.S. industrial relations: the joint labor-management committee. Indeed, a comparison of these two forms of participation can be instructive since they are likely to focus on different issues and have different effects on workers, unions, and the larger bargaining relationship. For this reason, one of the cases reported in this study is a labor-management committee. We will use that case to highlight the differences in these two forms of participation.

Worker Participation
and American Industrial Relations

One might ask, why should representatives of the labor movement even question the benefits to be gained from efforts to increase worker participation in decisionmaking at the workplace? Shouldn't any process that serves to increase the voice workers have in issues that affect them be consistent with the goals of labor unions? An answer to these questions requires a grounding in the history and basic features of the American industrial relations system and the role and status of labor unions in American society.

Since the passage of the National Labor Relations Act in 1935, the American industrial relations system has been designed around the premise that collective bargaining is the preferred channel for worker representation and participation at the workplace. The American system of collective bargaining is based on the concept that a duly certified union is to serve as the exclusive representative of workers. As the exclusive representative, a union has the right to negotiate with management over a clearly defined, but limited, scope of issues pertaining to wages, hours, and working conditions.

This legislation emerged out of a political and social environment that had previously been quite hostile toward the rights of workers to organize to protect their collective interests and to participate in decisions at the workplace. Support for the rights of workers to organize and be represented by national unions (i.e., unions whose membership base extends beyond the boundary and control of the employer) arose only after the collapse of the American Plan in the 1920s. The American Plan consisted of a mix of strategies providing limited participation rights to employees through informal committees or company unions dominated by the employer.[1] The plan and employer resistance to unions were weakened by successful organizing drives by industrial unions in the 1930s. Thus, the power and stability offered by a legally enforceable collective bargaining contract and an independent collective bargaining agent were achievements that American workers and their labor unions fought hard to achieve in the 1930s and have valued ever since.

Since the 1930s, collective bargaining has served as the basic institution by which American workers have enhanced their economic security and expanded their sphere of influence at the workplace. This incremental expansion of collective bargaining contracts was achieved through hard bargaining supported by the bargaining power achieved largely through the threat of the strike.

Although collective barganing has expanded in scope since the 1930s, American unions have never been genuinely accepted by American management as valued partners in industrial relations. The prevailing American managerial strategy continues to be, on the one hand, to avoid unions wherever possible, and on the other hand, to deal constructively with unions wherever they exist or cannot successfully be avoided.[2] This management strategy, along with a deeply ingrained belief that social and economic gains can only be achieved through struggle and hard bargaining, has produced a sense of insecurity and distrust of employer motivations among many American labor union leaders. While the above statements may overdramatize the conditions under which the American industrial relations system and U.S. labor unions have evolved, they set the context for the reception received by early efforts to introduce QWL concepts to American unions.

Early Responses to QWL

QWL theory in its simplest form is based on the proposition that through collaboration and cooperation of workers and employers the quality of working life experiences of individual workers and the goals of employers can be simultaneously enhanced.[3] While this is a laudable objective that would be difficult for anyone to oppose, more careful examination of the way it was introduced to American unions helps us to understand why it was viewed with considerable skepticism by the majority of labor leaders.

In order to understand the initial response of the American labor movement to early proponents of QWL theories and strategies, we need to look at the origins of those theories and their mode of introduction to American unions. While the theoretical underpinnings for QWL strategies can be traced back to early human relations theory,[4] for our purposes we need only look back to the late 1960s and early 1970s when the term QWL first became part of the American vocabulary.

Furthermore, early proponents of QWL largely ignored the history of industrial relations and collective bargaining outlined above. While industrial relations recognizes the need for *both* hard bargaining and mutual cooperation,[5] the behavioral science theories upon which the QWL advocates derived their strategies ignored the conflict side of the employment relationship and stressed only the need for and value of cooperation. In their crudest form, the behavioral science theories were really theories *of management* developed *for managers* rather than theories of the employment relationship from which policies and practices could be derived for balancing the diversity and maximizing the commonality of interests at the workplace.

Labor union representatives were quick to point out that these behavioral science theories left no significant role for labor unions as representatives of workers. Indeed, most behavioral science and QWL applications found their homes in nonunion companies and were used as part of the union avoidance strategies of these firms.[6] Thus, many observers within the labor movement saw the QWL strategies as simply another in the long list of efforts of American employers to weaken the labor movement.[7] In essence, QWL was perceived as simply the American Plan revisited. The values of openness, high trust, extensive communications and participation of individuals which the behavioral scientists emphasized were seen as simply another way of avoiding the need to deal with collective bargaining.

Consequently, QWL started off in the U.S. with a poor image among labor unions. It did not help that the early proponents of QWL experiments also tended to oversell the concept as a solution to the "Lordstown" syndrome. That is, in the minds of the QWL advocates, the problems facing American workers in the late 1960s and the early 1970s were that workers were alienated from their work because they were closed off from meaningful opportunities to influence their working environment. This alienation allegedly was the cause of excessive levels of absenteeism, wildcat strikes, and the blue-collar blues. In addition to diagnosing the problem in this way, the QWL advocates also had a ready-made solution, namely, to experiment with a predesigned QWL program and thereby begin to address the "real" needs of American workers.[8] Little thought was given to how these new strategies for participation would relate to existing collective bargaining and industrial relations systems. Nor were systematic efforts made to assess the extent to which unions, through collective bargaining, were in fact effectively responding to the priorities of their members. Correspondingly, the reception given to the early QWL efforts was quite cool from union, and even from many management, representatives.

But despite this rocky start, some highly visible experimentation did take place in the early 1970s under the auspices of the National Commission on Productivity and Quality of Working Life with the support of research and consulting expenses provided by the Ford Foundation. These government- and foundation-sponsored experiments were complemented by a variety of private initiatives in both nonunion and union plants. The early experimental sites have now become household names within quality of working life circles. The most frequently discussed experiments occurred in the Rushton Mining Company, General Motors Tarrytown plant (and subsequently many other plants of General Motors), the Bolivar, Tennessee plant of Harmon Manufacturing Company, the Topeka General Foods pet food plant, and several others.[9]

While many of these highly visible programs faded away by the latter part of the 1970s (especially those sponsored by the government), they were succeeded by a much broader array of private experiments that emerged near the end of the decade and in the early 1980s. This second generation of experimentation was fueled by the deepening economic crisis affecting American industry, the growing awareness of the stagnant productivity trends experienced in the American economy in the 1970s, and the increasing attention given to Japanese management practices by the American mass media. Indeed, according to one set of estimates, in early 1982 approximately 1,000 companies had Quality Circles under way, 100 companies had more advanced forms of work reorganization experiments involving autonomous work groups and another 500 or so companies were engaged in Scanlon Plan type (productivity gains sharing) projects.[10] In recent years, interest in various forms of participation has clearly diffused to a wider spectrum of firms and unions. Perhaps most significantly, a number of international unions have negotiated clauses into their agreements that launched joint union-management participation experiments. The most notable examples are found in the contracts between the United Automobile Workers and the major auto firms, the United Steelworkers of America (USW) and eight major steel producers, and the Communication Workers of America (CWA) and AT&T.

The Current Context For Worker Participation

This brings us to the current debate within labor union circles. Clearly, there is now a much wider diversity of views within the American labor movement concerning the viability of quality of working life processes than was the case in the previous decade.

At the same time, fear and suspicion still exist among many unions and workers regarding QWL programs. The basic fear expressed by opponents or critics of worker participation programs is that their ultimate effect will be to undermine the strength and effectiveness of the local union and the collective bargaining process. Specifically, critics have argued that: (1) workers and/or employers may see these processes as substitutes for, rather than as supplements to, the collective bargaining process and established grievance procedures; (2) workers may begin to question the need for a union if they see employers listening to and solving their problems through QWL or other direct worker participation processes; (3) union leaders may become too closely identified with management or get co-opted into managerial decisions, lose touch with their members, or experience heightened internal political instability or conflict; and (4) informal participation processes may turn out to be simply another short-lived strategy for employers to gain greater control over and effort from workers without providing them with any real power to influence important decisions within the firm. Finally, since these efforts are often used by nonunion employers as part of their union avoidance strategy, some labor leaders see these processes as inherently antiunion in design.

Supporters of worker participation processes generally argue that the negative consequences outlined above can be avoided by proper union involvement in the design and implementation of participation programs. Supporters also stress that many employers will be experimenting with these processes regardless of whether or not the union is involved. Remaining outside of the process or being involved in only a minimal way will further erode the status of the union at the workplace. Others argue that support for worker participation should be more than a defensive reaction to employer initiatives. They believe unions should embrace worker participation processes as strategies for extending industrial democracy to individual workers. Finally, some union advocates believe that, by making worker participation processes an important part of the broad agenda of the labor movement, unions will enhance their attractiveness to new workers in future organizing campaigns.

Theoretical and Analytical Issues

The central theoretical argument running through our analysis of these issues is that worker participation processes move through several stages of evolution as they unfold. It is only by understanding the dynamics of these processes through time that we can hope to understand their effects on local unions and on the larger collective bargaining relationship and assess the arguments of the QWL advocates and critics.

It is particularly important to follow workplace experiments through at least one complete contract cycle, i.e., from the initiation of the experiment to at least one follow-up negotiation of the collective bargaining agreement. This allows us to observe how the participation process affects and is integrated into the larger collective bargaining relationship. In addition, to test the stability or survival power of these experiments, it is necessary to watch what happens to them over time as business conditions change, key management and/or union supporters turn over or hand over responsibility for the project to others, union leaders who support the process stand for reelection, and other problems or conflicts in the bargaining relationship arise. Then, exploring how union member and officer views and experiences change over the cycle of collective bargaining, we can better understand whether these experiments are temporary fads which have a natural but rather limited "half-life," or represent changes in the workplace industrial relations system that have lasting effects. The organization of the chapters follows this approach. We first present case study descriptions of the evolution of worker participation processes over the course of at least one contract cycle and often through changes in the economic circumstances of the parties. In chapter 3 we explore the especially complex issues that arise in sustaining worker participation processes operating under centralized collective bargaining structures. In centralized structures, many more interests and decision-makers within both management and union can influence the course of a participation process thus taking the control over the process partly out of the hands of local officials. We are fortunate to have two well known cases to draw on for this analysis, the United Auto Workers and General Motors and Ford, and the United Steel Workers and the major steel producers. Then, we examine through survey and interview data the views that rank and file members, and local labor leaders hold toward worker participation.

Models of the dynamics of a joint union-management change process have been presented elsewhere and need not be repeated in detail here.[11] It may be useful, however, to summarize the general points of consensus found in these models since we use them to structure the analysis that follows. As noted above, the common argument in models of organizational change, and particularly in models of joint union-management change, is that once a change is started, the process takes on a dynamic character. Thus, it is important to trace the effects of worker participation processes from the initial stimulus to change, through the early stages of implementation, and on to the stage at which the informal participation experiments are "institutionalized" or once again integrated into the larger collective bargaining relationship. The basic propositions in these models are as follows.

(1) Introducing a worker participation process generally involves considerable political and economic risks to both management and union officials. Normally, therefore, both parties will only begin to explore the idea of starting a worker participation process if they feel intense pressures to do so. These pressures may come from external markets, legal, social, or political sources, or from internal sources such as from the expectations and preferences of workers or top managers. Furthermore, the parties can expect to encounter considerable skepticism and some resistance to these changes from workers and managers alike.

(2) To generate a joint initial commitment to proceed, both parties must perceive the process as being useful for achieving goals that are important to *their respective organizations or constituencies.* That is, management must see the process as having the potential to improve organizational effectiveness and union leaders must see the process as enhancing economic or psychological goals or needs to which workers assign high priorities. Broad appeals to the general, long-run or mutual welfare of the parties will not provide sufficient incentive to diffuse the process to large numbers of workers.

(3) Maintaining commitment to the process over time will be difficult. It will require overcoming the internal political opposition which is likely to arise from some workers, union leaders, and/or managers. It will require successful attainment of the initial goals of the process, and will require continuation of the pressures that initially stimulated the change. In short, like all forms of labor-management cooperation, worker participation processes are fragile instruments.

(4) Ultimately, continuation of the process over time will require: (a) attainment of tangible goals valued by the workers and the employer, and (b) "institutionalizing" the changes into the ongoing collective bargaining relationship.

NOTES

1. For a discussion of the American Plan see David Brody, *Workers in Industrial America* (New York: Oxford University Press, 1980).

2. Thomas A. Kochan and Robert B. McKersie, "Collective Bargaining: Pressures for Change," *Sloan Management Review* 24 (Summer 1983).

3. Elton Mayo, *The Human Problems of an Industrial Civilization* (New York: Macmillan, 1933).

4. For a clear statement of this purpose see Paul S. Goodman, *Assessing Organizational Change* (New York: Wiley, 1979), pp. 7-8.

5. Jack Barbash, "The Elements of Industrial Relations," *British Journal of Industrial Relations,* 2 (1964), pp. 66-78. See also Thomas A. Kochan, *Collective Bargaining and Industrial Relations* (Homewood, IL: Irwin, 1980), pp. 1-23.

6. Fred Foulkes, *Personnel Policies in Large Non-Union Companies* (Englewood Cliffs, NJ: Prentice Hall, 1980).

7. See, for example, William Winpisinger, "Job Enrichment: A Union View," *Monthly Labor Review* 96 (April 1973), pp. 54-56.

8. One book that was perceived by many to have adopted this theme was *Work in America* (Cambridge: MIT Press, 1972), a report of a Special Task Force to the Secretary of Health, Education, and Welfare.

9. For a recent review of most of these key experiments see Robert Zager and Michael P. Rosow, eds., *The Innovative Organization: Productivity Programs in Action* (New York: Pergamon Press, 1982).

10. Jerome M. Rosow and Robert Zager, eds., *Productivity Through Work Organizations* (New York: Pergamon Press, 1982).

11. See, for example, Thomas A. Kochan and Lee Dyer, "A Model of Organizational Change in the Context of Union-Management Relations," *Journal of Applied Behavioral Science* 12 (1976), pp. 59-78. See also Michael Schuster, *Union-Management Cooperation: Structure, Process, and Impact* (Kalamazoo, MI: W. E. Upjohn Institute for Employment Research), forthcoming.

Chapter 2

Dynamics of Worker Participation Processes
Single Cases

This chapter will present five case studies which illustrate the dynamics of worker participation processes. Particular attention will be given to how experiments which may begin as relatively narrow efforts focused on involving individuals and small groups of workers in decisions affecting their jobs can expand and influence the larger collective bargaining relationship. By drawing on a number of different cases we will also demonstrate that there is no one single outcome or path that participation processes follow. Rather, a wide range of positive and negative outcomes has been experienced by different unions at different points in time.

Local 14B and Xerox

The first case discussed in this chapter is that of Local 14B of the Amalgamated Clothing and Textile Workers Union (ACTWU) and the Xerox Corporation. We will report the experiences of these parties in some detail since this case nicely illustrates many of the central themes developed in this book. Specifically, the case illustrates the fit between a QWL process and the larger economic, organizational, and collective bargaining context in which the process is embedded.

This case involves a large, highly skilled, blue-collar bargaining unit located in the Rochester manufacturing facility of Xerox. The union and the company began a jointly administered QWL program in late 1980 after a clause authorizing experimentation with such a program was included in their 1980 bargaining agreement. Data for this study were gathered through interviews with the parties over a three-year period starting just after the initiation of the QWL process and ending after the settlement of the parties' 1983 labor agreement. Survey data were collected from a sample of 387 workers out of a bargaining unit of approximately 4,000 workers. The case data were collected during the summer of 1982, approximately 20 months after the start-up of the QWL project. In this case, the union involved in the QWL project acts as a full joint sponsor and sits with representatives of management on all of the various steering and oversight committees. The actual participation process resembles a Quality Circle (QC) program.

Background and Environment
for the Experiment

Local 14B and Xerox have had a long-standing, cooperative collective bargaining relationship. The company voluntarily recognized the union in the late 1940s when the firm was a small manufacturer of a single product line. From the outset, the relationship was influenced by the strongly held philosophy of the founder of the firm. He believed in the desirability of maintaining cooperative and highly professional relationships between the union and the company. His commitment has carried through the relationship up to the present time and his philosophy was passed on to his various successors in later years, largely through the continued leadership of the director of industrial relations for the Corporation.

In the 1950s, Xerox began to capitalize on a series of technological breakthroughs that transformed the firm from a small and largely unknown business to one of the leading Fortune 500 corporations. The company continued to enjoy rapid rates of growth and high profits through the 1960s since its technological advances had continued to provide a near monopoly in the major product line. As the company expanded, new plants were opened and the union was voluntarily recognized on the basis of card checks or uncontested representation elections in each new facility. The major manufacturing facilities of the Corporation are located in one medium-sized city in the Northeast. Smaller facilities are located in other cities in various regions of the country. The company also acquired several smaller firms within the last decade as it sought to diversify into related product lines seen as having higher growth potential than the products on which the company's previous growth was built.

The competitive environment for this company changed dramatically during the last decade. Both domestic and foreign competition intensified at the same time that the growth in the overall market for its products began to slow down and decline toward the end of the 1970s. The market decline continued at an even more rapid rate during the recession of the early 1980s. By 1982, the company announced that it would be necessary to reduce its blue- and white-collar labor force by at least 30 percent as it struggled to regain its competitive position in its basic product line and to slowly but surely shift its new product development resources to the newer, more promising lines of business it had developed through acquisitions in recent years. Thus, the QWL process in this case exists in a bargaining relationship that historically was characterized by higher levels of cooperation and an economic environment that had turned from one that had been expanding for a long period of time to one that was rapidly deteriorating.

Origin and Structure of the QWL Process

The QWL process was launched with a provision included in the parties' 1980 collective bargaining agreement. That provision reads as follows:

Employee Involvement

A Joint Company-Union Employee Involvement Committee shall be established to investigate and pursue opportunities for enhancing employees' work satisfaction and productivity. To this end, the Joint Committee shall meet regularly to undertake the following responsibilities:

A. Review and evaluate ongoing programs, projects, and experiments, both within and outside the Company, designed to encourage employee involvement.

B. Develop programs, projects, and experiments that might ultimately be broadly applied.

C. Establish subcommittees to develop suggested programs for specific areas. Hear and review reports from these subcommittees.

D. Submit reports and recommendations to the Company and Union regarding the implementation and subsequent progress of specific programs.

The original idea for this provision came from the chairman of the board of the company. He indicated an interest in developing some type of employee involvement program. Both the industrial relations staff of the Corporation and the international union representatives were prepared to discuss this issue in negotiations since both groups had been examining the experiences of other companies and unions with various worker participation experiments during the year prior to the beginning of formal negotiations.

Program Structure and Content

The structure used to implement the QWL process consists of several different joint committees and groups. At the top of the structure is the Planning and Policy Committee which consists of four union officers and four management representatives including the vice-president of manufacturing, the manager of personnel, the manager of industrial relations, and the manager of QWL services. This committee meets approximately every four to six weeks and is responsible for establishing broad guidelines and policies for the QWL process. Each of the four central plants in the company's major manufacturing complex has an Advisory Committee consisting of 10 union and 10 management representatives. The job of these advisory committees is to develop plans for implementing the QWL process and monitoring its progress and coordinating its activities with other developments in the plant. Within each plant the various business centers also have a steering committee consisting of the manager of the center, two foremen, two technical personnel, and four union representatives. The task of this committee is to provide support for the QWL teams that undergo training in problemsolving techniques.

The basic unit of the QWL process is the QWL team. Each team consists of six to eight employees from the same work area. Participation in a team is voluntary; however, both bargaining unit and other employees are encouraged to participate. Each team elects its own leader who may or may not be the supervisor for that work group. Approximately 50 percent of the leaders in these groups are not supervisors.

Each team undergoes an initial 40-hour training program of which 28 hours are paid for by the employer and 12 hours are contributed by the employee. The training program is spread over approximately a 10-week period and emphasizes problemsolving skills and team building. Figure 2.1 illustrates some of the material typically covered in a training program. At the end of the training program, a graduation ceremony is held in which each team presents its analysis of workplace problems and suggested solutions to the management of that plant. Union representatives normally are present and speak at these graduation ceremonies.

Figure 2.1
Putting QWL into Practice
Problem Solving Team - Education & Training

QWL/EI Concepts

Problem Solving Skills
- Data gathering techniques
- Cause and effect analysis
- Pareto analysis and histogram
- Check sheets and control charts
- Using statistics

Team Building and Functioning
- Interpersonal communications
- Effective team meetings
- Team records and reports
- Work on real problems
- Using technical staff support
- Presentation skills

Program = 40 hours (28 paid, 12 voluntary)
: 4 hours over 10 weeks

Graduation - team presentations on real problems

Presented to: steering committee and management

After graduating, each QWL team meets once a week for approximately one hour to discuss problems and to review the status of suggestions for improvements made at previous

meetings. The groups cannot make changes that would conflict with the provisions of the collective bargaining agreement. The parties refer to items which are "on line," i.e.,
those issues which fall within the legitimate scope of discussion of a QWL team, and "off line" issues which are
covered by the collective bargaining agreement and therefore
cannot be altered by a specific suggestion from a team.

The efforts of these teams are supported by eight full-time
union and eight full-time management QWL coordinators.
The coordinators provide technical advice and help train the
teams. Each coordinator has agreed to remain in this position for at least two years. In addition, a full-time manager
of QWL services monitors the overall program for the Corporation. He is assisted by an outside consultant who initially worked approximately four days a week with the union
and the company and now has scaled his involvement down
to approximately one to two days a week. The hiring of the
consultant was also a joint activity of the local union
representatives and the company. In fact, the first individual
to be considered was replaced by the present consultant
because both the union and the management representatives
felt that the present person was more successful in developing a rapport with union officers and committee members.

The teams can be accurately described as Quality Circle
groups. The focus is on problemsolving around job-related
issues. No changes had been made in the organization of the
work, the roles of supervisors, the compensation structure,
or other structural aspects of the plant level work organization as of June 1982. The manager of QWL services,
however, saw this as only the first phase of a more
amibitious organizational change process. In addition to increasing the number of workers trained for the QWL process
(his goal is to train and involve 80 percent of the workforce
by the end of 1985), this manager sees the process moving on
to the point where workers and QWL teams would address a

wider array of issues related to work organization, job design and work layout, and work group management. This would move the QWL process closer to an autonomous work group type of organization. As of the summer of 1982, however, none of the teams had moved to this stage nor had the company and the union agreed to this objective.

By the summer of 1982, approximately 25 percent of the members of the bargaining unit had been trained and were participating in a QWL team. Because the company has been experiencing layoffs since mid-1981, a number of people who have completed training are not participating in teams because the teams have been disrupted by movements of people through the seniority bumping process.

Initial Union Response to QWL

According to the international representative of this union, the officers and members of the local were not sure how the QWL process would affect them. He stated:

> We weren't making a quality product and we knew if we could produce a better product it would enhance job security. But the stewards were skeptical, the shop chairmen didn't want to get involved. They didn't know what QWL meant and it was a gimmick to them. The company has had *so* many programs each beginning and ending at various points in time. At the same time, the union's perception of the company's goals at the outset of the program was that this was an honest approach to get workers involved in improving efficiency and quality. We thought that the top executives of the corporation (the Chairman of the Board and the President and Chief Executive) were sincere.

Thus, despite some initial apprehension, the union decided to go ahead, include the language in the agreement reported above, and actively participate in the development and implementation of the program. A year after the initiation of the QWL process, the key union representatives reviewed their own views of the process to date. The international union representative stated that:

> This has been a real eye opener to me. Management wanted to make certain changes and produce more to meet their schedules. The workers agreed to cooperate. They understand the competitive threat better now. They see the relationship between their work and the success of the product they make.

The business agent for Local 14B has been with the company for more than 15 years and was also quite skeptical of the program at the beginning. He assessed the status of the program one year into its life as follows.

> Management is really sharing information with us. This would not have been possible three or four years ago and I see this as a result of the QWL program. At a meeting yesterday, for example, the vice president of manufacturing shared all the numbers on costs and future orders that he has so we could really get behind this layoff problem. [The union representatives and the company had met to try to avoid the layoffs of approximately thirty people and had been successful in doing so.]

Another long-time company employee and union official is the general shop chairman. He is currently a full-time employee paid by the company. In addition to being responsible for coordinating the work of the shop stewards, he is the key union representative who oversees the QWL process. He started out as a strong skeptic of the QWL program but later became a strong supporter. He stated, for example,

> At first I saw little point in all of this. We worried that this sort of program would make the shop stewards superfluous. But we have had no regrets.

The program is running very efficiently. The management director of the QWL program is very fair in his dealings with the union. We have had great confidence in the consultant that the company hired to work with us and we trust him. The key is that we are considered to be equals by management. It's not like a short-lived program run by management where we will be left to pick up the crumbs.

The support of the shop stewards was a bit slower in developing in this case, as in most cases. Still, however, when we interviewed them at two years into the process, none of the shop stewards voiced opposition to the program, none saw serious overlaps or jurisdictional conflicts between the QWL process and the handling of grievances or with provisions of the collective bargaining agreement, and all of them agreed that the union should continue to support the QWL process and be actively involved in it. Consequently, the first two and one-half years of the QWL process was a time of growing support and commitment on the part of top union leaders and union stewards. In addition, the union representatives serving as QWL facilitators were emerging as another important group of union activists supporting the process.

Evolution of Management Support

As noted earlier, the initial impetus to the QWL process came from the chairman of the board of Xerox. Within one year of the negotiations over the 1980 agreement, this chairman was scheduled to step down and be replaced by the current president of the Corporation. This president and future chief executive officer also shared a strong commitment to develop the QWL process. Thus, the commitment from the top levels of the Corporation was very strong at the beginning of the program and remained strong through its initial implementation phase.

While support at the top had been strong from the start, support at the plant level and among middle managers was reported by both company and union representatives to be more variable and problematic. The first real test of the continuity of the program came near the end of the first year of the program. At that time a new vice-president of manufacturing had just taken over, and the budget for the second year of the program was under discussion. At the same time, the company was experiencing increasing competitive pressures and it was clear that layoffs would be coming in the second year.

The issue of funding and cost of the second year of the program came to a head in a meeting that involved the managers of the four plants in the manufacturing complex, the vice-president of manufacturing, the QWL consultant, the director of QWL services for the Corporation, and the three key union officials discussed above. The meeting began with the vice-president indicating that the estimated $6 million price tag for the second year of the program was too high, that the money was just not available for the program. The outside consultant reported the dynamics of this meeting from that point on as follows:

> The dynamics of this meeting were interesting in two respects. First the General Shop Chairman (who is the union representative on the QWL program) took on the new Vice President of Manufacturing and challenged him directly by asking him if the company was "decommitting" to the program. Second, the plant managers took a much more active role in challenging the new vice president as well and in trying to look for alternative solutions. The General Shop Chairman initially brought up issues that the plant managers should have raised themselves such as, what's the consequence of backing off the program the first time money becomes an issue?

These discussions ultimately produced an agreement that the plant managers agreed would absorb some of the costs of the second year of the program within their own line budgets and would look for ways to bring the cost of the program down without slowing its progress. Eventually the cost of the second year was pared down to $3 million as opposed to the original estimate of $6 million. Consequently, with the joint support of the local union representatives and the line managers, the QWL process survived its first initial test, the turnover of a key management decisionmaker.

The lack of support for the program from middle managers and first-line supervisors was recognized by all of the parties. Indeed, after two years of experience with the program, the QWL manager was asked by the vice-president of manufacturing to develop a strategy for dealing directly with the lack of support from middle managers. They titled the new strategy "Changing the Management Culture."

Local union representatives estimated that perhaps 80 to 85 percent of the line managers above the first-line supervisors and below the plant managers were opposed to the QWL process. Opposition of these managers was attributed to their fear of losing power and having their roles changed while they failed to see the leadership styles and decision-making processes of managers above them changing in ways that were consistent with the QWL process. Opposition also appeared from some support groups such as the manufacturing engineering personnel who felt threatened by the idea of having hourly workers suggesting changes in work practices or layouts that had heretofore been within the jurisdiction and discretion of engineering.

Evolving Views of the Rank and File

Rank and file employees explicitly agreed to initiate the QWL process when they voted to ratify the 1980 collective bargaining agreement. Although that agreement was ratified by an overwhelming margin, the QWL provision included in the agreement did not play a significant role in the discussion of the contract or in the vote itself. Thus, the first real evidence available concerning rank and file reactions to the QWL process came from the response to initial requests for volunteer participants. According to both the manager of QWL services and union representatives, there was some initial reluctance on the part of most employees to be the "first to get involved." Just as the union representatives indicated in their statements, rank and file members had already seen a number of management initiatives to improve productivity or try out a new communications program or enhance attitudes and were fearful that this was another "gimmick." However, a number of groups were convinced to consider the process. After the first several groups responded very positively to the QWL training, interest in the concept spread more easily and rapidly. The manager of QWL services reported that after the program was initiated and several teams had completed training, most requests for volunteers resulted in a positive response from 50 to 70 percent of the employees in a work group.

There were clear signs, however, that rank and file interest in participating began to decline during the second year of the program. The general shop chairman reported that by the midpoint of the second year of the process, it was getting more difficult to get volunteers to participate. Indeed, when we conducted our survey two and one-half years into the process, only 25 percent of those not yet participating indicated a willingness to join the QWL process. Moreover, analysis of the perceptions of those involved showed that those who had gotten involved early in the process were beginning to express more negative attitudes toward the union's handling of QWL issues. (More detailed analysis of the survey data is found in chapter 4.) These quantitative data were reinforced by the statements of the general shop chairman. In discussing our survey data he stated:

> Those numbers seem to coincide with what I
> thought was going on. Those who got involved ear-

ly are saying to us "We took some big risks in getting involved early. Then we see that we are improving productivity and quality in our shops. At the same time layoffs are occurring all around us and the workforce continues to shrink. We are now asking what are we getting out of this process."

Links to the Larger Collective Bargaining Relationship

The experiences surrounding two events illustrate the relationship which emerged between the QWL process and broader collective bargaining issues. The first event concerns a high labor cost operation that the firm was threatening to subcontract to outside vendors. The second event is the process and results of the negotiation of the 1983 labor agreement, the first agreement to be negotiated after the QWL process had been in effect.

The High Cost Operation. One of the most difficult and controversial issues to arise between the company and Local 14B in the last several years has been the question of what to do with approximately 200 workers involved in the manufacturing of wiring harnesses, an electronic component that goes into the overall product. When Xerox first developed the technology for its copying machines, no other firms had the capability of manufacturing the necessary types of harnesses. Therefore, the company developed this capability in-house and has always produced its own wiring harnesses. Yet, as this technology became more routine and the market for these parts grew, many new small firms entered the market and sold these components to larger firms for use in their final products. Almost all of these newer and smaller firms are nonunion and pay wages considerably below the rate paid for unionized employees covered under the Local 14B agreement. Indeed, the average total wage and fringe benefit cost for Local 14B employees in this particular operation in 1982 was approximately $19 per hour, compared to estimates from one vendor of $8 and another of $12 per hour. Productivity comparisons also failed to show any significant offsetting advantage to the Local 14B employees. Consequently, many managers within Xerox had been arguing for several years that wiring harness operations should be subcontracted to an outside vendor. The pressure to do so was intensified by the fact that all of the firm's domestic competitors that had entered this market considerably later than Xerox were currently subcontracting this component to outside vendors. Thus, the cost of this particular part of the manufacturing process was considerably higher for Xerox than for its competitors.

This problem had been recognized by both the industrial relations staff of the Corporation and the local union leadership for a number of years. Indeed, an agreement had been worked out prior to 1980 to slowly phase out the manufacture of wiring harnesses but to do so without laying anyone off. This agreement became unworkable, however, as the market for the firm's products began to deteriorate in 1980. Therefore, the union and the company recognized they needed to return to this issue in search of an alternative arrangement. While there was strong pressure within management to simply contract out the work, there was strong opposition to this proposal from the local union. The vice-president of manufacturing described the discussions that ensued around this issue in 1981 as follows:

> Management three levels above me made a decision to close down this operation. The international representative of the union responded to that decision by pointing out that his shop stewards were just livid about this decision because it contradicted an earlier negotiated effort to reach an accommodation on this problem. As a result several of us within management said ''Let's not just put these people out on the street but let's give the problem to them to see if something can be worked out. Let

the people themselves select a team to decide what is needed in this area." So this is what we did.

A group of workers and supervisors organized a task force to examine alternatives for reducing the costs of operations in this area. After one year of study and research the group came back with a number of, as the vice-president of manufacturing described them, "astonishing recommendations." Below is his description of what the task force recommended.

> The group found that management was doing a number of things wrong. The layout of the plant was wrong and they showed how it could be redesigned. The amount of overhead allocated to this area of the plant was also found to be wrong. They found lots of things that could be done differently. For example, they want to alter the contract language governing transfers and promotions to slow down the movement of people across jobs. They would like to have a separate seniority unit for people working in this area to also cut down on the number of moves in and out of the operation. They would like to fix the jobs so that people don't desire to rotate out of them but make them more flexible and interesting. They would like to use more part-time workers at peak periods of production to smooth out the workforce and to allow the payment of lower wages and fringe benefits. They propose eliminating a number of supervisors and working as a semi-autonomous work group. Overall, they have come up with a twenty-nine percent cost reduction proposal. Companies can't get twenty-nine percent cost reductions these days through management studies alone.

Obviously the changes proposed by this group strike directly at the heart of the collective bargaining agreement. The union and company representatives studied these recommendations, accepted those that did not significantly alter the bargaining agreement, modified several in ways that did not cause significant problems for the agreement, and agreed to put those that required major changes in the bargaining agreement on the table for negotiations during the next round of contract talks.

This example illustrates a point that comes out in all the cases we examined in this research, namely, that it is difficult to draw a hard and fast line of demarcation between the QWL or worker participation process and the collective bargaining agreement. While the contract language governing the QWL process clearly provided the boilerplate "shelter agreement" provision stating that nothing in the QWL process would alter the provisions of the agreement, it is clear that as groups such as the one described above begin to explore alternative arrangements for organizing work, reducing costs, or increasing productivity, their explorations are very likely to lead them directly into contractual provisions. As long as the participation process is limited to specific Quality Circle types of activities, it may be possible to limit discussions to topics described as "on line" and to avoid those "off line" topics that are the province of the bargaining agreement. Over time, however, it is likely that this distinction will become more difficult to enforce, as was the case in this example. At the same time, it does not necessarily mean that solutions cannot be identified that both preserve the integrity of the bargaining agreement and do not frustrate the change process. As we will see, the key to the parties' successful handling of this issue at Xerox was that they clearly recognized the need for union and management representatives to *negotiate* those issues that did involve contractual language.

The 1983 Contract Negotiations. Contract negotiations for the first agreement after start-up of the QWL experiment began in late 1982 in anticipation of a contract expiration date of March 31, 1983. Both parties knew that this was going to be the most difficult negotiations they had faced in more than 30 years. Since the 1980 contract was signed, the market for the firm's products had shrunk drastically, the recession of 1981-83 had depressed sales across the industry, and the firm had embraced a new business strategy of attempting to compete on the basis of price for the first time in its history. These changes in competitive conditions and strategy necessitated deep price discounts which in turn put intense pressure on manufacturing costs. The firm also made a decision to permanently reduce its blue- and white-collar labor force by over 30 percent, with the heaviest concentrations in workforce reductions coming in the manufacturing facilities where the QWL process was in place. Furthermore, the concession bargaining that had dominated negotiations in many other industries in 1981 and 1982 meant that many of the industries and unions traditionally used as bases of comparison had already implemented contract concessions and wage deferrals. Finally, accompanying the transition to the new business strategy and the increased pressure on manufacturing and labor costs, came a shift in the distribution of power within top managerial circles. The power of the financial cost-conscious managers had increased at the expense of industrial relations. As a result, the industrial relations staff lost much of the autonomy it had previously enjoyed over the planning and strategy formulation for labor negotiations. Thus, the union representatives recognized that other management officials were in direct control or "calling the shots" for these negotiations and that the industrial relations staff would be under intense pressure to negotiate labor cost reductions and tighter contractual language.

Just where concern for the QWL process stood within management as negotiations opened was in serious question. The union representatives believed that the hard-line position advocated by management negotiators signaled that the company really did not care about whether the QWL process survived these negotiations or not. They felt that the company was being hypocritical in the approach it was taking to negotiations. On the one hand, all during the term of the agreement the company was preaching the values of QWL with its stress on openness, problemsolving, high trust, and information sharing. On the other hand, when it came time for negotiations, the company's initial proposals called for major concessions in the areas of subcontracting language, job transfers and promotions, and other sensitive areas. In addition, the employer representatives appeared, in the eyes of the union negotiating team, to take a rather closed-minded approach to negotiations rather than indicate a will-ingness to consider alternatives in a problemsolving fashion.

The union, for its part, opened negotiations by making two basic points. First, it stressed that it had cooperated with the company throughout the term of the agreement to develop and sustain the QWL process and that it wanted to maintain and strengthen that process. Second, it stressed that in order for the process to be sustained through a second term of the contract, some provision for job security and for sharing the gains of the QWL process needed to be included in the new agreement.

The parties eventually reached an agreement after extend-ing the old contract two weeks beyond its scheduled expira-tion date. Four provisions included in the new contract are relevant to the QWL process:

1. The parties agreed to continue the QWL process with no significant changes in the language governing this pro-cess.

2. The parties agreed to extend the wiring harness experi-ment to all subcontracting situations. That is, if the company proposes to subcontract out work that it believes is not currently being done at a competitive level, the issue will first be given to the QWL team in that area to see if it can propose a strategy for making the operations competitive. If the work is contracted

out, the company agrees to bring in other work that can be performed at competitive costs. Any worker assigned to this new work will retain his current rate of pay.

3. The company agreed to a guarantee of no layoffs for the three years of the new agreement.

4. All remaining issues involving the wiring harness area were resolved.

This agreement represented a major step toward the integration of the QWL process with collective bargaining. Essentially, the process of experimentation with new work organization (the wiring harness proposals) was generalized to all similar situations and made a part of standard operating practice. In addition, the union achieved the job security guarantee (at least for the term of this agreement) believed needed to maintain rank and file and leadership support for the QWL process. Finally, those issues which the parties were not able to settle through the QWL process because they were too central to the overall bargaining agreement were appropriately referred to the bargaining table and resolved there as part of the overall renegotiation of the agreement. Thus, without judging the merits of the specific terms agreed to by the union and the company, this case serves as a model for linking the QWL and collective bargaining processes.

Summary and Conclusions

This case illustrates how a narrowly focused agreement to experiment with a QWL process evolved over time in the face of changing economic circumstances. It grew from an effort to improve the QWL experiences of individual workers into an integral part of the parties' strategies for addressing the basic economic problems of the firm and the job security concerns of the union membership. Innovations first suggested by participants in the QWL process have since been transformed into standard operating procedures. The QWL process survived its first set of severe tests because the parties successfully responded to the job security concerns that had caused worker support for the QWL process to plateau and decline.

While the parties were successful in this case in negotiating an agreement that reinforced the QWL process in the face of an extremely harsh economic environment, these negotiations could just as easily have led to the demise of QWL and a return to a lower trust, arms-length union-management relationship. The high level of trust built up over the years between industrial relations professionals and union leaders in this company were clearly instrumental in seeing the parties through these difficult times.

Local 717 and Packard Electric

The QWL process between Local 717 of the International Union of Electrical Workers (IUE) and Packard Electric is the longest running worker participation project in our sample. Since Packard Electric is a division of General Motors, the development of a QWL program at this company is not independent of the origins and history of QWL in the auto industry. As will be outlined below, however, the content of the program has gone considerably farther than most of the QWL activities described elsewhere in this book. Indeed, this case provides the best example of a local union that saw the QWL process right from the beginning as a strategy for protecting job security. Thus, there has always been a close link between the QWL process and this union's broader strategies for representing the basic economic interests of its members.

Background to the QWL Process

The beginning of the QWL process can be traced to an announcement made in 1973 by the general manager of Packard that there would be no more hiring or major capital investment in Warren, Ohio due to the high cost of production. As a result, job security became a major concern to the Packard employees during the mid-1970s. The current union administration, although not in office at that time, ran in 1977 on a platform to save the workforce through closer cooperation with management.

Evidence that the joint efforts were viewed as a means of addressing concerns over job security can be seen in the following statement by the chairman of the shop committee who was elected in 1977.

> Between 1956 and 1973, Packard had grown to 13,500 employees. Between 1970 and 1973, we still hired but in 1973 started to implement a long-range strategy. . . . so highly labor-intense production was subcontracted and new plants were opened in the South. In 1975 I was not the Chairman—I had been defeated—so I went back to the machine for two years. Working there and listening to the people gave me good insight as to what people wanted. In 1974-75 started the industrial decline and the biggest concern was job security—[the workers] felt the threat. There was a lot of emotion in the plant. [The President] and I got together in 1977 and ran on the platform that we would try to save jobs and have closer cooperation with management; that, yes, the union and its people could have an impact on the future. When elected, I began to implement that.

After that union election, weekly labor-management meetings were initiated involving the shop chairman, president of the union, plant manager, and personnel director. That group, or the Steering Committee as it was later called, started its joint efforts with several noncontroversial joint projects, such as blood drives, the collection of funds for United Way and the Employee Assistance Program.

At about the same time as the Steering Committee was formed in 1978, a management task force was created to improve the performance of Packard in Warren. The shop chairman then offered the union's participation in that group and the result was a joint union-management Jobs Committee. The purpose of this committee is to:

> . . . develop an ongoing union-management approach that will maintain job security and identify opportunities for hiring in the Warren operations.

In addition to saving and creating jobs, the Jobs Committee is concerned with employee involvement in Packard's operations. The joint committee operates by examining various methods for saving and/or creating jobs and then develops projects to accomplish that purpose. These projects tend to address operational problems such as improving quality, production or product delivery.

As noted above, employee involvement is included in the philosophy of the Jobs Committee. While it is difficult to separate the formal "quality of working life" activities from the projects initiated by the committee, a wide spectrum of employee involvement or worker participation projects at Packard Electric has been started since 1978.

The Jobs Committee

As noted earlier, one of the objectives of the Jobs Committee is to build the concept of worker participation into the projects it undertakes to save and/or create jobs. That committee consists of eight union and eight management representatives. The union members include the president, shop chairman, two subchairmen, two committeemen, one benefits representative and one skilled trades representative, while the management representatives consist of members from each staff area. In order to illustrate the accomplishments of the Jobs Committee, three successful projects from 1978 and 1979 are briefly described below.

(1) The Maintenance Survey Project—Four new employees were hired as a result of this project. Its purpose was to identify ways to improve construction performance. Two teams observed construction-

maintenance personnel, noted how time was wasted, and recommended the purchase of machinery and tooling and the creation of new jobs.

(2)   The Metal Parts Project—A team of employees was organized to reduce costs in the metal parts area so the company could successfully compete for metal parts business on a worldwide basis. The team recommended the purchase of several new presses, which resulted in a cost reduction and the subsequent hiring of 46 employees.

(3)   The Skilled Trades Requirement—As a result of the branch plants' operations, office expansion, projected requirements and experience gained from the previous two projects, the Jobs Committee recommended that 115 new jobs be filled in the skilled trades area. The result was the hiring of 115 people.

Between 1978 and 1980 the Jobs Committee participated in the decision to hire employees as well as the purchase and construction of three new plants in the Warren area. In recent years, however, the committee has had a more difficult task, since the company announced late in 1981 that 3,900 jobs in Warren were noncompetitive and had to be eliminated. In response to that announcement, the Jobs Committee began to search for alternatives to layoffs. As a result, it reduced the workforce by 900 employees through accelerated attrition programs. A voluntary termination of employment program and an early retirement program were developed and the parties are currently in the process of establishing a part-time workforce. All of these ideas were developed in the Jobs Committee and subsequently taken to the bargaining table and agreed upon during 1982 negotiations.

Committees of Hourly Employees

By the summer of 1983 there were approximately 60-65 committees of hourly employees operating. While all these committees could be classified as QWL groups, in fact their scope and functions vary considerably. The parties classify the committees into four groups: (1) "Non-Risky" Committees, (2) Task Forces, (3) Employee Participation Groups and/or Statistical Process Control Groups, and (4) Semi-Autonomous Work Groups. The types of hourly committees are listed and then defined below in order of increasing worker involvement.

The "Non-Risky" Committees deal with "safe" topics such as health and safety, housekeeping, and substance abuse within a work group. A greater level of involvement exists in Task Forces, which usually are offshoots of the Jobs Committee. A Task Force searches for causes of problems identified by the Committee and then recommends solutions.

Employee Participation Groups or EPGs (similar to Quality Circles) are voluntary groups of 8 to 12 employees who typically meet once a week for an hour to discuss work-related issues, identify problems and search for causes and solutions. Statistical Process Control Groups or SPCs are groups of employees using the company's concept of SPC, which basically is a statistical system of identifying control limits for defects as opposed to traditional inspection. SPC is not perceived by everyone to be "worker participation" but the employees in a work group are involved in the process as a team.

Three production lines in one of the new plants operate as Semi-Autonomous Work Groups without a direct supervisor. These employees are involved in the most extensive form of worker participation.

Summary

As in the Xerox case, at Packard it is impossible to draw a line between the collective bargaining strategies and activities of this local union and its worker participation strategies and efforts. Improving the quality of working life was not the driving motivation behind the development of joint efforts.

The driving motivation was, and still is, to save jobs by making the operations performed by these workers more competitive. The various worker participation efforts and the joint union-management committee structures that oversee them are *means* used to achieve these economic objectives. Thus, the Packard case brings our argument full circle. In the previous case we documented how QWL efforts gradually move into the traditional territory of collective bargaining. In the Packard case, the process moved in the opposite direction as the parties carried traditional topics of negotiations into the worker participation process.

Local 2 and the Uniform Piston Company

This case illustrates the pitfalls of a narrowly focused Quality Circle type of program that operates largely in a vacuum, without consideration for the larger set of events occurring in the collective bargaining relationship between the company and the local union. We will call this the case of Local 2 and the Uniform Piston Company (disguised name) since the company is a small manufacturer of auto parts employing a bargaining unit of approximately 300 semi-skilled and unskilled workers.

Background to the "Group 33" Program

The worker participation program at this company evolved out of a "jobs evaluation committee" formed by the company and the union during the summer of 1979. The original committee met to discuss problems and make recommendations concerning the general work environment in the plant. When people realized that this committee created the type of communications that should be encouraged throughout the organization, the concept of work teams (called "Group 33s") covering the whole company was developed. As a result, a central QWL Committee was created as an umbrella group to encourage the formation of work teams. It is important to note, therefore, that in this case the QWL process evolved out of an informal labor-management committee's decision to experiment, not out of a clause negotiated into the collective bargaining agreement.

Program Structure and Content

The members of the central QWL Committee are a cross section of the various interest groups in the organization so that different departments, ages and sexes are represented, as are both union and management. In addition, current members of the committee have all served as QWL facilitators for the Group 33s at some point in time.

Group 33s are considered by the organization to be "people building tools." Their name is derived from the three phases of a person's life: community, work and home. The goal is to improve all three phases of the employees' lives through the teaching of problemsolving techniques at work. All participation is voluntary and groups are formed when people volunteer.

The Group 33s operate under the same guidelines and philosophy as does the QWL Committee. Each Group 33 meets to discuss mutual problems and to develop solutions as often as necessary, but meetings are limited to one hour per week. If the entire group agrees, it will work on any problem that does not interfere with the negotiated contract or involve any of the following subjects:

— wages and salaries
— benefits
— disciplinary policies
— employment policies
— termination policies
— personalities
— company rules

Although there is no formal training for Group 33s, facilitators spend two to four weeks working closely with new groups in order to familiarize the members with the

QWL process. Facilitators can be either union members or salaried personnel and are selected by union officials and management representatives. Facilitators also return to groups periodically to ensure their progress.

Union Views of the "Group 33" Process

Twenty-five percent of the workers in the bargaining unit were participating in Group 33s in September 1982, one-and-one-half years after the start of the QWL process. Interviews with the local union officials indicated general satisfaction with the status of the QWL process. However, a number of clouds appear on the horizon of this program. The problems did not spring from what is occurring in the groups or within the QWL process itself, but were a consequence of the weak presence of the local union in the administration of the QWL process and in the larger strategic decisions being made by the company. We will draw on our interviews with the local union representatives to illustrate this problem.

Separation of Problemsolving from Union-Management Relations. While the union is formally involved in the QWL structure, the actual role of the union is more one of a "watchdog" than an active partner. As a result, the activities of the local union appear to be limited largely to issues that involve conflicts and disagreements with management, while the QWL process is becoming identified as the central forum for cooperative problemsolving. Thus, the union is associated with largely adversarial issues and the more informal QWL process is given credit for solving problems. The following quote by the vice-president of the union illustrates the difference in management's attitude toward him when he raises an issue in the QWL process compared to when he raises an issue as a union official.

> When I come in to QWL Committee meetings I'm an *employee* working to solve a problem. The QWL Committee is easier [than formal union-

management meetings]. The people from the company are not against [the union] right off the bat—they're willing to work with us with no problem. If we disagree with them in QWL, we discuss it. But as a *union,* if we disagree, then they get mad and leave—they hold grudges and it filters out into the shop. . . . Management is more honest in the QWL program than they are with union problems overall.

The separation between the QWL process and the handling of contractual items was further illustrated by a problem that occurred when one of the QWL groups made a proposal for an employee evaluation system. This proposal was forwarded to the QWL Committee, which in turn forwarded it to management, which in turn approved it. The union, however, viewed this new proposal as an infringement on the collective bargaining agreement and thus rejected it. This proposal arose at the time the company and the union were negotiating the 1981 contract. The net result was that the company and the union did not agree to include any language on this issue in their new agreement. Subsequently, however, the company unilaterally implemented part of the employee evaluation proposal outside of both the collective bargaining agreement and the QWL process.

Both the local union and management representatives agreed that this employee evaluation proposal and its handling had a negative impact on the QWL process. The management representative responsible for the QWL process indicated that this controversy almost "wiped out" the participation program. The president of the local union said that the union was "almost ready to throw QWL out of the plant" because of the proposal. Since management approved the proposal, the union president viewed QWL as "a union busting tactic." He resigned from the Group 33 of which he was a member in December 1981 because of this controversy.

The company and the union did reach an accommodation in negotiations over the 1982 contract on the issues deemed to be outside the jurisdiction of the QWL process. This convinced the local union officials that management's objectives for the QWL process were legitimate and the union subsequently dropped its objections to the continuation of the QWL process. The union president expressed his feelings after these negotiations as follows:

> They're not touching our contract as far as we can see. . . . Management is asking employees about quite a few things. I don't think they are trying to pull anything over the union any more. They know they couldn't get away with it.

The Opening of a Nonunion Plant. Another issue surfaced in early 1982 when the company opened a new nonunion plant in a southern state and subsequently began laying off employees in the northern unionized plant where the QWL process was underway. This was only the second layoff experienced by employees of this company in over one hundred years. The president of the union expressed his lack of trust in management as a result of this development as follows:

> The company took a lot of our work out of the plant and put it in the new plant in the South and now they are working and we have people laid off. The people out here aren't trusting management on a lot of things. . . . If we'd still had that work that is being done in the South, those people would not have been laid off.

Implications of this Case

This case illustrates a number of potential pitfalls for a local union that can arise out of a worker participation process that is not linked to the collective bargaining relationship through contractual language at the outset and where the QWL process at the workplace is isolated from the larger strategic decisions of the company. If the QWL process takes over more of the problemsolving functions at the workplace, the union is left with a more limited agenda of adversarial issues that it can claim as its own. New ideas, such as the employee evaluation proposal, which generate enthusiasm among a subset of employees, then create the appearance that the union is only an opposition force. Finally, this case is an example where an employer is asking its local union and union members to cooperate at the workplace in the short run while it is in the process of making a strategic decision to divert investments to a nonunion plant in another part of the country. Because the local union officials are not directly involved in the design and administration of the QWL process and have not used the QWL process to open a dialogue with company officials over strategic decisions, the union is not in a position to link efforts to preserve jobs to the participation process.

Local 70 and Freeman, Inc.

A Case Study of a Demoralized QWL Process

This case summarizes the quality of working life efforts at Freeman, Inc. (disguised name), a major Canadian grocery chain. QWL programs were initiated in several of the grocery stores in Freeman's Ontario division and in a new meatcutting plant also located in Ontario.

Freeman operates approximately 75 stores in the Toronto metropolitan area, all of which are organized by the same international union (we will refer to this union as Local 70). In late 1981, the company also opened a new meatcutting plant just outside of Toronto on the same property as the Ontario division headquarters. This plant is also organized by Local 70. The union participated jointly with the company in designing the plant on a socio-technical basis. The plant ran for approximately eight months on that basis but it lost money and operated at an unacceptably low level of productivity and quality. As a result, the company decided to bring in a new plant manager and revert back to a very traditional management and organization style and work organization system.

The QWL program in the retail store division predated the opening of the meatcutting facility by about three years. Four stores were involved in some form of QWL process at one time or another. Experience with these QWL efforts encouraged the company to use the socio-technical design to set up the meatcutting facility. In 1981, the company began experiencing severe financial pressures, largely due to the recession and to the increase in competition from independent grocery stores and other retail outlets. Partly because of this pressure and partly for other reasons, QWL programs in the stores faded out of existence. In short, this is a case study of a demoralized QWL program both in the retail stores and in the meatcutting plant.

Background to the Meat Plant

In the late 1970s, Freeman's management decided it was necessary to build a meatcutting and packaging facility. The general manager indicated that the decision to set up the plant on a socio-technical design and to work jointly with the union was made right at the outset. He stated,

> We saw an opportunity to design a plant with a new approach. We wanted to do it on a quality of working life and socio-technical system basis. We saw this as an extension of the QWL philosophy that we were developing in our retail division.

Union and employer representatives visited meat facilities in the United States. The union also received advice from its international union concerning the designs and blueprints for the plant as they were developed.

The personnel manager for the plant indicated that, although the union was involved right from the beginning, its involvement was generally limited to reacting to designs as they were drawn up. In other words, the union took little initiative in developing its own ideas or suggestions. There was also a tapering off of union involvement about half way through the design phase, according to the personnel manager. He believed that the union's involvement in the design of the plant was consistent with its posture in relation to other QWL efforts:

> Instead of committing themselves to joint decision-making they preferred to take the position of "you show us what you plan to do and we will tell you if it's okay." Instead of taking a joint design approach, the union prefers to maintain its veto authority role.

The union representatives indicated that they did have full opportunity to participate in the design of the plant and that they had confidence in the outside consultant hired by the company to help install the new work system. Indeed, the key union business agent involved in the QWL efforts indicated that she was very satisfied with the role that the consultant played and his efforts to insure that union points of view were taken into consideration.

The Design and Operation of the Plant

The plant cost approximately $27 million to build and equip. Approximately $1 million of equipment was placed at the front and the back end of short manufacturing lines, whereas a traditional plant would have had much longer lines and required only about $500,000 of front and back end equipment. In a traditional meatcutting plant with long lines, jobs are very highly specialized. In this plant there were five short lines with fewer specialized jobs. In addition, the lines were designed to allow workers to move across different operations more easily.

The work was organized around work teams of 12 to 16 people with the goal of having everyone learn all the different jobs in the plant. There were to be no dead-end jobs in the plant and no discrimination based on sex or race in the allocation of jobs to different individuals. Furthermore, the jobs were designed in a way so that the physical requirements did not exclude any individuals from any jobs. For example, in a traditional meatpacking plant, beef carcasses arrive in railroad cars or trucks and require considerable hoisting at all stages of the front end operations. In this plant there was no heavy hoisting except at one point where the carcass had to be raised up to the first saw. Conveyors and mechanized hoisting were built into the design to allow women and other individuals with less lifting power to work on jobs at the front end of the plant.

In traditional plants there are finely defined job classifications with the meatcutter being the topmost skilled classification. Payment is based on the job being performed at a particular point in time. The design of this plant called for people to progress through the six levels of the job classification system by learning the various jobs and being certified as being capable of performing the different tasks. The system design called for "pay for knowledge" rather than pay for the work performed.

The original design called for very few managers and no traditional foremen. Instead, work was organized in work teams on an autonomous work group basis with facilitators providing assistance and help in organizing the work. The collective bargaining agreement governing the first year of operation in the plant was a very simple and short document. It covered the economic terms of the contract but did not contain detailed provisions on seniority, bumping, or other job classification and work organization provisions. Instead, it provided that the progression system would be monitored by a review board which also handled recommendations, grievances, discipline cases, and other issues. The review board was made up of three workers and three managers from the plant, and the union business agent.

Experiences Under the Socio-Technical System

According to the personnel manager, the workforce had a mixed reaction to the initial organization of work in the plant. The greatest sources of resistance came from the most skilled meatcutters. The personnel manager indicated that in the traditional organizations, meatcutters prefer to work with red meat, i.e., beef rather than poultry or pork. Some of the top flight butchers who earlier had transferred from the company's stores to the plant resented the idea that they had to rotate around to less skilled jobs and that other people could be working in the high skilled classifications without going through the long periods of training and seniority accumulation that the butchers had gone through. According to the personnel manager, the top butcher also tended to be a "rough tough type guy" who served as an informal work group leader.

In addition, in the past there were few women in the skilled jobs in meatpacking operations because of the heavy lifting and dangerous nature of the work. Finally, the idea of conducting team meetings where the authority and status of the top butcher or meatcutter was being challenged made it difficult for some of the workers to adapt to the new organization. On the other hand, many employees had an opportunity to learn new jobs and obtain new skills in the plant at a very swift pace. As a result, the overall reaction to the new arrangement was mixed.

Problems with the Work System Design and Implementation

The company expected to lose approximately $8 million in the first year of plant operations. However, in the first eight months it had already lost $20 million. Productivity and product quality were both very poor in the months that the plant was operated under this system. The business agent in charge of the plant indicated that she saw many problems developing in the plant, both with the way in which the workers handled their newly found ambiguity and freedom, and in the general operation of the plant. Some of the workers, according to the business agent, took the new arrangements as "a license to steal." For example, workers took longer coffee breaks, the team meetings failed to focus on substantive workplace issues and accomplished little, and in some cases workers even rigged up a bogus reporting system where at one point nine workers were falsely reported to be at work. Workers were also being certified at classification levels well beyond their ability. These are only examples of the more extreme problems which developed under the system.

After the plant had been operating for eight months, the top executives of the corporation made a decision to replace the plant manager and to abandon the socio-technical work system. Interviews with the managers and union officials involved suggested the following reasons for the failure of the new system. First, it is clear that management made a major mistake in failing to staff the plant with managers experienced in either general manufacturing or meatpacking manufacturing. Instead, all the managers of the new plant came from the retail food operations and brought retail orientations and experience into the factory environment. Thus, they did not understand either the technical or the social system they were getting into. Second, although there was a well-articulated design for the social side of the plant, the consultants lacked knowledge of the technical nature of a meatcutting plant. Their prior experience in implementing socio-technical systems came from other manufacturing environments. Third, inadequate workforce training was provided regarding problemsolving techniques, workers' responsibilities under the new work organization and semi-autonomous system, and management's expectations for production.

The Change to a Traditional Operation

The regional director of Local 70 believes the central reason for the failure of the socio-technical program was that people took advantage of the freedom offered under the system. In addition, he believes that the management was afraid of the union in the plant. He said, "They went along with anything the union wanted and didn't know how to manage this type of plant environment." Essentially, he reinforced the earlier statements that management was not prepared to manage this type of participatory system. In addition, he stressed that the company made a serious strategic mistake at the same time they were trying to get this new meat processing plant off the ground. The company had changed its marketing strategy by opening discount stores and cutting prices. At the same time prices were being lowered considerably to fit the discount model, the new meat processing plant was starting up and delivering meat of substandard quality to the supermarkets. Thus, the customers associated the drop in prices with lower quality products and the company's previous high reputation rapidly declined.

Eventually new plant management turned the organization back to a traditionally-run operation. Team meetings were eliminated. Any meetings are now conducted under direct management control. In addition, time clocks were installed and production lines were sped up. Job rotation was stopped.

The Aftermath of the Socio-Technical System

Six months after the shift to the traditional organization and management system, the union and the company completed negotiations over a successor agreement to the one-year contract used to establish the new plant. The union had originally planned to introduce only a very short list of contract proposals and modifications to the skeleton agreement that governed the plant for the first year. The new management, however, according to the business agent, "forced us to cover our ass." Therefore, the union proposed a traditional collective bargaining agreement. It essentially brought

all of the standard seniority, job classification, union security, management rights, and other work organization clauses
back into the plant agreement. The management organization was quite "shocked" at this approach since it preferred
to maintain the skeleton agreement. However, the final
negotiated agreement did contain most of the standard contract language. In the future, the company would still like to
have some form of team organization and would like to retain the quality of work life aspects of the earlier experiment,
but not go back to the overall socio-technical design.
Management also is now determined to maintain traditional
management controls and supervisory roles in any future
participation effort in order to avoid the problems experienced under the experiment.

The Views of the General Manager

The key driving force in the development of the QWL efforts and the socio-technical design of the meat plant was the
vice-president and general manager of this company. He was
a very strong supporter of the QWL concept and believed
that the key to the future of labor-management relations lies
in the development of a high-trust relationship. His comments on the QWL efforts and the experience with the meat
plant, in an interview shortly after the start of the negotiation of the second year contract, are outlined below.

> My overall opinion of where we are with our
> QWL efforts is that with all the excellent things
> that we have accomplished we are fundamentally
> failing. We have not yet rid ourselves of fear and
> distrust of each other. Fear and distrust are under-
> mining our ability to bring about meaningful
> change. This distrust is leading to the negotiation
> of a new labor agreement in the same old way that
> we negotiated earlier agreements instead of
> building on the positive experiences we have been
> trying to develop. Instead, the union is responding

this time the same way it has in the past. I can understand this because of the way we have handled the socio-technical plant and the way we have now had to regress in our operations there.

Our hope is after we do this we can go back to our original intentions. Basically what we need to do is to eventually get on to some core issues in our relationship with workers and with the union to open ourselves up to real significant change by unfreezing our relationship. I was really disappointed in our inability to move on to core issues and bring about change.

I believe after all I have been through so far that we will not get significant change until we jointly agree to confront the market changes and what they imply for employees. We can't be afraid to use our vision and take risks. We have to stop faking around the issue of productivity and recognize that we are in a mature industry. We have to educate the union and employees to know what the retail life cycle is all about and to recognize and realize that there will have to be change if we are to survive in this industry.

Views of the Business Agent

The business agent responsible for the plant generally agreed with the view that the change to a more traditional management system was needed to get the plant operating efficiently and profitably. At the same time, she remained strongly committed to the belief that some form of worker participation, if properly structured and managed, should be designed into future plans of the union and the company. She stated her specific views as follows:

We have to look into these ideas and develop them. Look at what happened here. Even though we had a disaster from the standpoint of the plant operations we had nothing to lose for trying and in fact no one has lost anything yet. No workers are worse off now than they would have been if we hadn't got into this effort.

In the future the union's role should be one that's focused more at lower levels of our organization. We should rely less on the involvement of people like myself as business agents and work much more with our stewards and members of plant committees. We cannot bring about change from the top down through the company union-management core group down to the plant level and to the stewards in the store or plant. We have to work from the stewards and the membership on upward. The union staff has to be more of a resource rather than a direct coordinator or manager of the program.

The Broader QWL Program in the Retail Stores

In addition to the failure of the socio-technical program, the broader QWL process in the retail stores that had been in place for several years fizzled out within the last year and a half. Again, the regional director of Local 70 stressed the interaction of the tougher economic times that the company faced and the internal political changes within management that led to the demise of the QWL experiments in the four stores. He described the issue as follows:

The problem was very much internal management politics. Middle management never really got committed to the effort. Especially the regional managers were not impressed or supportive.

The regional director went on to describe the politics at the top of the company as well:

The whole QWL concept started because Fred Freeman was behind it [the chief executive officer and chairman of the board and the family head who controlled the corporation]. Fred sold the idea to the former president of the company and he sold it to three or four of the other top people in the company but this was still only less than half of the top key management officials. Then Fred died and the direction of the program was left in the hands of the other board of director members who were less enthusiastic about the idea in the first place. The other board members were not part of the family but approached the process from more of a professional management standpoint and were much more focused on dollars, profits, and productivity. Therefore they panicked much quicker when the program began to experience problems and the company began to go through this period of tough competition and losses.

Aftereffects of the Demise of QWL

When asked whether there were any traces of the QWL or socio-technical programs left on the union as an organization, both the regional director and the business agent responded that there were no adverse consequences. They said, "We can honestly say that nobody was ever hurt by the QWL efforts." In fact, they believe that some very positive by-products came out of the process. They stated that they are the only union that was able to negotiate a guarantee of jobs for full-time workers in the stores and they attribute this directly to the improved climate and relationship that came out of the QWL process. They also saw some progress toward solving long-standing problems for night crews by bringing them into the mainstream of the company and giving them an opportunity to get onto the day crews for the first time. However, these efforts also fizzled somewhat as the QWL process eroded.

Summary

In summary, this union's experience with both the QWL and the socio-technical design process illustrates that a union can experiment with worker participation efforts and manage its way through the demise of these efforts without any lasting negative consequences. This union did so by maintaining sufficient distance from the design of the program so that it could always react to what the company was doing and be involved in it, but not be out in front leading the effort. The union, on the other hand, did not have control over the rise and fall of the process, nor could it contribute to the avoidance of the disastrous consequences that it saw occurring under the socio-technical system. Consequently, this is an example of the case where the union was both a junior partner in success and in failure. The parties are now back working under a standard contract and carrying on in traditional collective bargaining fashion.

Newspaper Guild and *Minneapolis Star* and *Tribune*

The Case of a Labor-Management Committee

In contrast to the other cases reported in this chapter, this case illustrates the unique features of an indirect form of worker participation, namely, a Labor-Management Participation Committee. In addition, this case stands out as our only example of a professional employee bargaining unit. It is the case of a major newspaper and a group of reporters and other newsroom workers represented by Local 2 of the Newspaper Guild employed by the *Minneapolis Star* and *Tribune.*

Background to the Worker Participation Program

A system of worker participation was formally proposed by the Newspaper Guild during 1972 negotiations. Management argued against it, saying it "wasn't necessary," but the

Guild succeeded in making the worker participation proposal a part of the contract. That provision called for a joint labor-management committee which would meet at least once a month and would discuss any topics it wished, with the exception of contractual matters. In 1976 the authority of the committee was extended to include problems arising out of technological change.

The Guild had first become involved in worker participation in 1971 when it consulted with management regarding the appointment of two assistant city editors. The position of assistant city editor is crucial to the efficient flow of the news system, a fact of which the Guild was well aware, especially after some "unfortunate" appointments were made to those jobs in the past. As a result, the Guild approached management with the proposal that the Guild have advice and consent authority over the appointment of the two assistant city editors. Although management representatives said they would not give veto authority to the Guild, the executive editor said he *would* be willing to consult with the Guild about these appointments as well as future appointments to supervisory positions.

Management and the Guild then had a meeting during which management discussed their candidates for the two positions and the Guild subsequently recommended two of those persons. It turned out that the Guild's choices matched those of management and those two persons were appointed. It should be noted that assistant city editors are part of the Guild's bargaining unit, so the Guild was participating in a decision which involved its own members. This was the Guild's "first taste" of what its members called "worker participation" and thus led to the Guild's proposal during 1972 negotiations.

Program Structure and Content

The structure of the worker participation process consists of a joint labor-management committee known as the

Worker Participation Committee (WPC) which meets approximately once a month. WPC members often form subcommittees for the purpose of investigating issues and researching solutions to problem areas. Each news department initially had a WPC, so there was one committee for the *Minneapolis Star* and one for the *Minneapolis Tribune.* However, the two newspapers merged in 1982, so that currently there is a single WPC. The merger and its effects on the worker participation process are discussed in a later section of this case.

Guild members of the WPC are elected annually by the membership and represent each area of the newsroom. The Guild's business agent also attends all WPC meetings, as an observer rather than as an active participant in the discussions. The editor-in-chief and assistant editor attend all meetings. The remaining management representatives who attend change from one meeting to the next. Each WPC thus consists of approximately 12 Guild members and a varying number of management representatives. In addition, any other interested members of both parties may attend a WPC meeting if they so desire.

Prior to the WPC meetings, the Guild members caucus to discuss possible agenda items. Then one Guild representative meets with a management member to formally set up the agenda. There is no formal process for soliciting ideas or suggestions regarding topics for discussion. However, Guild members are encouraged by the WPC representatives in their area to bring up any issues they wish, and Guild representatives regularly take informal polls to solicit topics for discussion. Minutes of the WPC meetings are posted each month on departmental bulletin boards and usually serve as a springboard for comments made by Guild members to their representatives on the committee.

During the WPC's 10 years of existence, it has moved from a kind of "grievance committee" for noncontractual matters to much more of a participative decisionmaking process for the Guild. According to the business agent, expectations of the Guild initially were "not too high," so that topics during the first couple of years primarily were based on complaints about necessary equipment for the newsroom and cafeteria food. Initial accomplishments of the Guild included the installation of a refrigerator for employees' lunches and showers for female employees.

One of the earliest "nongrievance" type of joint decision by the WPC which greatly increased its visibility concerned the strategic direction of the afternoon paper. In response to the question "What kind of paper shall we be?" the WPC agreed that the strategy should be to become a state paper.

The "acceptability" of the WPC was proven in 1974, when negotiations did not involve an attempt by management to weaken the language of the worker participation provision. As both management and the Guild became more comfortable with worker participation, the WPC meeting began to include broader issues. Management also started giving the Guild annual departmental budget figures.

As a result of 1976 negotiations, the language regarding worker participation was changed in order to give the WPC authority over any problem concerning technological change. This was regarded as a significant accomplishment by the Guild, since the newspaper industry was beginning to undergo massive changes in technology—the use of computer terminals and VDTs was drastically changing the way of life in the newsroom. Due to the revised provision, the Guild secured permission to bring in a consultant to measure for radiation, and management agreed to buy glasses for job-related cases of eye strain.

During the past five years, the WPC has been involved in a substantial number of newsroom issues. The following is a list of topics discussed at WPC meetings during which Guild members contributed ideas and recommendations:

— policy on confidentiality of sources
— how additional news space might be used
— writing seminars
— seminars on law and newspaper reporting
— newsprint
— staff size
— orientation program for new staff members
— free lance policy
— office redesign
— criteria for selection of editors
— parking
— minority hiring program
— promotion campaigns
— by-line policy
— readership projects
— circulation problems
— schedules for reporters

Current Status of Worker Participation

The Merger of the Newspapers. The merger of the *Star* and *Tribune* in the spring of 1982 had a dramatic impact on the Guild members and WPC. The merger resulted in the layoff of 70 people, 54 of whom voluntarily agreed to resign with a year of severance pay. Since prior to 1982 only four Guild members had been laid off for economic reasons (and subsequently reinstated through arbitration), the layoff due to the merger was a severe blow. However, it was the manner in which management handled the merger that was viewed as damaging to the Guild: the WPC was *not* allowed to participate in deciding the details of the merger prior to its occurrence. Each Guild member of the WPC who was interviewed agreed that the merger had a "negative" impact on the WPC. One stated, for example:

> Everyone knew the Tribune was in trouble and it was just a matter of time before the papers were merged, but no one knew whether it was 3 months, 5 months, or 5 years. It was about 4 or 5 months before the merger that [the editor-in-chief and head of the management side of the WPC] . . . went to some of the people on the WPC and said, "Listen, there may be some changes coming down, we may have to merge some special sections and things like that. What I'd like to do is sit down with you and have the Worker Participation Committee help plan this." And in the meantime, [the editor] was working with some of the top people in this organization to merge the two papers *completely,* and never told us a word about it! All of a sudden, it comes to a day we find out, "Hey, the papers have been merged." So it was just a complete sham and that was just something in terms of how [management] saw the Worker Participation Committee in making important decisions at this place.
>
> And so that left a bad taste in the mouths of a lot of people about the Worker Participation Committee and the process that I would say *still* hasn't gone away. It was like a great breach of faith, we felt, on the part of management. . . . and it was very difficult to conceive of continuing the committee at that point.

Thus, even a process that has survived for almost a decade can be seriously threatened by one visible action by management (or, for that matter, by the union) which is perceived to be inconsistent with the trust relationship that has been built up by the participation process. This example illustrates the fragile lifeline upon which the continuity of worker participation processes rests.

Problems in the Worker Participation Process. In addition, many of the Guild WPC members who were interviewed were concerned about several other problems regarding the committee and the future of the process. The majority believed that a primary concern was the personality of the editor-in-chief, who acts as the chairman of the WPC meetings. The significance of his philosophy, particularly regarding his efforts to limit the scope of influence of the participatory process, is shown by the following statements about the WPC made by Guild members.

> [Management] holds the cards—*they* decide what the committee will do. They have complete power over it. The committee will do only what management will allow it to do. . . . but as negative as I've been . . . my problems are more with simply [the editor] and the way he ran this committee, rather than the idea itself. I think it can work . . . it *should* work . . . it's a good idea, even the way it's set up now. Even with the way [the editor] runs it, it's better than nothing, just in terms of simple communication. At least you're airing those views. . . . [The WPC] is valuable, but it's just gotta be done with the right person. And with the wrong person, it can be very, very frustrating. It probably *can* even become useless. I don't think ours was, but it was certainly very frustrating.

Another problem with the committee, according to some of the Guild members interviewed, is the length of time required to accomplish something. One member attributes that difficulty to adversarial relations:

> Because there's a tendency to see [the WPC] as an adversarial situation, it seems that there's too much time spent defining things. It's getting into details that really aren't that relevant. And it results in a sort of reluctance to try new things. That's one of the comments I've always heard about the com-

mittee every since I began to work here—is that it takes *forever* for anything to get done. And having sat on the committee, I can see why—there's a lot of rhetoric on both sides, there's a lot of smoke-screening, a lot of devil's advocacy. All of that I don't particularly enjoy. I don't see why people just don't lay their cards on the table—"There it is, let's decide what would be to everyone's mutual benefit."

This comment points out two facts that are often overlooked by the most vocal advocates of worker participation processes. First, true participation by people with diverse viewpoints generates debates, disagreements, and open conflicts. While participation processes must encourage the building of trust and problemsolving, they do not necessarily mean an end to conflict and negotiations. Second, involvement in participation processes inevitably produces some degree of stress and frustration among participants with the pace of decisionmaking and change. Democracy can be the enemy of decisiveness!

Evolution of the WPC

The future of worker participation for the Newspaper Guild members was believed to be "up in the air" by the WPC members who were interviewed. First, the impact of the merger has caused the Guild members to feel "betrayed" and led some to distrust management's motives. Second, a new editor was to joint the staff shortly after we completed our interviews and committee members believed that the WPC's functioning would be highly dependent on that person.

In addition to the changeover to the new editor, others recognized the need for the committee to continue evolving by addressing bigger, more important issues.

I think that the committee has evolved, to a certain extent, from what it started out to be, and I

think that to remain healthy, it has to change some
more. I don't know the degree to which that is going to be acceptable to management, but I'd like to
see it take on some bigger problems. That isn't
something, I think, that management has an interest at this point in agreeing to. But that again
depends on the kind of person, the kind of people
who are involved in management. If the people
who are there from top management are the people
who favor a reactive, bureaucratic sort of organization that . . . kind of discourages the sharing of
that sort of responsibility, then I think that we're
probably going to see a slide backward.

The business agent is determined to keep the WPC functioning, as shown by the following statement.

Not to let [the WPC] fail is our number one goal.
As long as the system survives, it will grow.

Summary and Conclusions

The WPC is a long-standing union-management participation committee that has survived several threats to its existence and has proven to be an effective supplement to the
collective bargaining process. Its primary impact appears to
be that it provides the Guild and its members with an ongoing forum for communicating with management and for
discussing issues of employer, union, and individual
employee concern that extend beyond the normal scope of
bargaining. As the survey data reported in chapter 4 will
show, these Guild members appear to see their union as being more effective in representing members' interests in
management decisionmaking on strategic topics than a comparison sister unit in the same local without any participation
process. It is likely that this is due, at least in part, to the
presence of the WPC.

Two implications emerge out of this case. First, it appears
that this type of organization-wide labor-management com-

mittee has improved the ability of this group of professionals to communicate with management and influence management decisionmaking on some strategic issues that are not possible to address within the formal collective bargaining process. Second, if there is interest in extending the concept of worker participation down to the individual employee, this type of indirect or organization level structure must be accompanied by experimenting with more decentralized and informal participation processes that bring small groups of employees into the process in a more direct way.

Summary and Conclusions—All Cases

The five cases of worker participation discussed in this chapter all demonstrate the difficulty of drawing a clear line of demarcation between the participation "experiment" and the collective bargaining process. ACTWU and Xerox and the IUE/Packard Electric cases suggest that to maintain momentum and support for the QWL process, the job security needs and interests of the workforce had to be met. In turn, the only way to maintain the interest and commitment of management to the QWL process was to find ways to integrate the process into the corporation's broader strategies for controlling manufacturing costs, improving productivity and adjusting to a more highly competitive environment.

The case of the Newspaper Guild demonstrated that even a labor-management committee that had survived for almost a decade was badly shaken and almost destroyed by a sudden management decision to merge two operations without prior notice or consultation with union representatives. Yet, the process survived this shock largely because union representatives and rank and file members see the participation committee as an integral part of their overall representational strategy. As one committee member put it, communications are not that good with the committee but without it they would be even worse and the union would not have any effective on-going channel to discuss issues that affect the professional interests of the workforce.

The case of Local 3 and the Uniform Piston Corporation illustrates the organizational and political pitfalls that a union is likely to experience when it adopts a "watchdog" rather than a "full partner" role in the QWL program dominated by an employer that is channeling investment resources into a nonunion plant. While no visible signs of trouble were evident to the union in this case at the current time, the seeds of destruction for the QWL process, and perhaps for the union itself, were firmly rooted in this situation.

Finally, Local 70's experience with a defunct QWL program and a failed experiment with a socio-technical work redesign operation demonstrates that even given the best intentions and good faith on the part of all parties involved, absent adequate worker training, management and consultant expertise, and a viable technical and market foundation for worker participation, the process is doomed to fail. Even given the failure of the socio-technical experiment, this case suggests that if both the employer and union recognize a failure when one exists and deal with it openly and in good faith, a stable traditional relationship can be reestablished without serious harm to either party. Indeed, by learning from the lessons of the failure, it may be possible to experiment with forms of worker participation again at some point in the future, albeit in a more cautious and thoughtful manner.

Perhaps the central lesson of these cases is that there is not a magical single line of steady positive results or improvements that automatically flow from a worker participation process. Each type of experiment is likely to go through periods of enthusiasm followed by skepticism and perhaps even disillusionment and decline. What appears to separate out those cases that survive is an awareness of the need to negotiate a way through problems and conflicts without destroying trust.

Chapter 3

Worker Participation Under Centralized Collective Bargaining

In this chapter we review the experiences of two major national unions with worker participation processes scattered across multiple plants as they moved through the difficult economic period of the early 1980s. Each case illustrates the challenges involved in linking workplace participation programs to the broader, more centralized collective bargaining structure and the broader strategies of the union and employers involved. The cases are: (1) The United Steelworkers (USW) and the seven major steel companies covered under the Basic Steel Agreement, and (2) The United Automobile Workers (UAW) and General Motors and Ford Motor Company.

The USW and the Steel Industry

The worker participation programs in the steel industry go under the label of Labor-Management Participation Teams (LMPTs). This program originated out of the 1980 collective bargaining agreement. The language governing this program (as amended slightly in 1983) states the intent of the LMPTs as follows:

> The strength and effectiveness of an industrial enterprise in a democratic society require a joint effort between labor and management at several

levels of interaction. The parties hereto recognize that if steelworkers are to continue among the best compensated employees in the industrial world and if steel companies are to meet international competition, the parties must pursue their mutual objectives with renewed dedication, initiative, and cooperation.

Collective bargaining has proven to be a successful instrument in achieving common goals and objectives in the employment relationship between labor and steel management. However, there are problems of a continuing nature at the level of the work site which significantly impact that relationship. Solutions to those problems are vital if the quality of work for employees is to be enhanced and if the proficiency of the business enterprise is to be improved.

The LMPTs can be viewed as a third generation labor-management joint venture in this industry. One of the early predecessors of this effort was the Human Relations Committee that was formed after the long 1959 steel strike. That Committee was composed of high-level company and union representatives and charged with the mission of developing a more cooperative relationship. While it was credited with improving the relations between union officers and company representatives, it was discarded in 1964 when I. W. Abel defeated David MacDonald for the presidency of the USW. Part of Abel's campaign was the contention that the union leadership had lost touch with the rank and file and it was time to return control of collective bargaining back to the membership.

A second generation of efforts to improve the relationship between steel management and the union and solve workplace problems was the formation of plant level Productivity and Employment Security Committees in the early

1970s. These were promoted by President Abel as a mechanism for improving the competitive position of the industry and the job security of the membership. These committees, however, never were well-accepted by plant managers or by local union representatives and this initiative quietly faded away by the mid-1970s.

By the time the USW and the major steel companies began negotiating their 1980 Basic Agreement, economic pressures were once again posing severe challenges to the industry and the union. The 1970s were a decade of rising import penetration in the markets of the major steel producers and growing excess capacity in the steel industry worldwide. In addition, the visibility of quality of working life efforts in the auto industry and the interest of several key union and management representatives led to the inclusion of the language quoted above in the 1980 agreement.

Thus, after the signing of the 1980 agreement, local unions in each plant and local managers could agree to experiment with the formation of LMPTs at their locations. Between 1980 and the negotiation of a successor agreement in 1983, 13 plants scattered across the seven companies covered under the agreement formed an LMPT program. In addition, during this time several companies and unions in the steel industry organized by the USW, but covered under separate agreements, established similar worker participation programs.

To examine experiences under this provision, interview data were collected from representatives of five locals with LMPTs and one local outside of the Basic Steel Agreement with a QWL program. Initial interviews were held with the local union presidents or representatives of these locals in the late summer of 1982 when the industry and the union were attempting to negotiate a successor agreement. The first attempt at an agreement had broken down and another attempt later failed before a new agreement was successfully negotiated and ratified by the USW in February 1983. Follow-up interviews were then held with several of the representatives of these locals after the signing of the successor agreement in order to trace their experiences through the negotiations.

As we review the experiences of these locals, it should be kept in mind that the LMPT program has been operating during the worst depression in this industry since the 1930s. At the time of our interviews in 1982, the industry was operating at less than 30 percent capacity and layoffs had reduced the workforce by more than 50 percent.

Initial Stages of LMPTs

The experiences of the first local to start an LMPT (and the most advanced and model project in the industry) illustrates the typical LMPT start-up process. This plant opened in 1903. Its peak employment was approximately 8,600 workers during the late 1970s. As of the middle of 1982, approximately 4,600 workers were employed within the bargaining unit. The plant had experienced major layoffs starting in October 1981. Although at that time four blast furnaces were operating, by February 1982 the company had scaled its operations down to only one-half a blast furnace and was producing only about 1,500 tons of steel per day.

Although there had not been any actual local union strikes in this plant in recent years, the local union president described labor relations prior to the development of LMPTs as highly adversarial. He stated:

> We always had a bad relationship. It was highly adversarial and each side thought the other side was not capable of bargaining in good faith. We did not have any strikes but a lot of our disputes went right down to the wire.

The LMPT program got started when Sam Camens, the USW international union representative who coordinates all of the unions' efforts in worker participation, asked the president of this local union if he was interested in starting a process based on the provision negotiated in the 1980 contract. The union president indicated his response was as follows:

> Of course I was quite leery of what the members would think. But because I was already viewed as a strong anti-company person it was easier for me to bring this idea to the members. The executive board was also at this meeting where Sam approached me about the idea. They took a very positive approach to the idea of getting involved.

> We started in May of 1981. We believe that the company saw as its basic objectives in this effort the improvement of productivity, quality, and the working relationship with the union. On our part, I was hopeful this effort would provide more dignity to workers, increase their input into decision making, ease the adversarial relationship between the foremen and workers, and give workers a feeling of participating in company and union affairs.

Structure and Operation of the LMPT Program

Most of the LMPTs are structured in the same general fashion. The president of the union, or a representative for the president, normally serves as co-chairman of a Steering Committee for the plant with a management counterpart. Often this management representative is the plant manager or the director of plant operations. The larger plants normally also have joint departmental or unit committees at lower levels of the organization. The work teams are the central unit within the LMPTs, normally consisting of between 7 and 10 workers and the supervisors located within a department. These teams normally meet one or two hours a week to discuss problems involving their work and review information on competitive costs, quality, productivity, and other data relevant to the performance of their group. In most of the programs, especially those progams supported by outside consultants, union and management representatives and the members of the work teams have received training on problemsolving. Team leaders are also often given additional training in group processes.

In all cases, care is taken to assure that the issues discussed by the teams and the suggestions offered do not violate the collective bargaining agreement. Union representatives on steering committees or on other committees above the level of the work teams monitor the suggestions coming from the teams to assure that they are not straying into contractual issues. From time to time, examples were cited in the interviews where the local union representatives had to inform the teams that they were talking about issues that were off-limits.

Gaining Initial Support Within the Plant

Each of the union representatives indicated that there was initial resistance to the program from a variety of sources within the union and within the plant. Active efforts to explain the program to union stewards, officers, and rank and file workers were needed in each location in order to overcome initial skepticism with which these groups greeted the idea of worker participation. Skepticism was greatest in those locals with the most active internal political opposition to the union leadership. For examples, in one plant where there had been a history of a "two party system" in the local, the union president described initial reactions of rank and file workers to the LMPT concept as follows:

> It depended on who talked to the members first. If those who opposed me politically talked to the members first the workers saw it as a company trick or another simple effort to increase productivity at

the expense of the workers. If I talked to them, then they understood the program as a reasonable idea.

In some plants the members of the union executive board were also initially quite cautious or generally opposed. In one case, for example, the executive board was initially split with half of the members fearing that the program would cut into their authority. Their approach, therefore, was to take the idea directly to rank and file workers, make it clear to them that this was a voluntary effort, and leave it to them whether or not they wanted to participate, without any endorsement or nonendorsement by the executive board. That approach, however, was the exception. In most other plants, after some initial discussion, a majority of the executive board endorsed the program. Over time, the support of the executive board typically increased as board members gained more experience with the program and rank and file workers reacted positively to the program.

Rank and file workers also were frequently somewhat skeptical at the beginning. Although the estimates of the degree of interest in the program varied from plant to plant, generally between 40 and 70 percent signed up for an LMPT team when given the opportunity. Most of the union representatives indicated that support for the process was strong among those workers who had been exposed to it, although there continued to be a good deal of skepticism on the part of rank and file workers who had not yet been involved. The most common response was that "Support is strong where we have it and people tend to oppose it where it doesn't yet exist."

In one plant, the union representative estimated that 90 percent of the workers were in favor of the LMPT process. This, however, is a very special case. In this plant, after the LMPT program was in progress for several months, the company closed the plant for a full one-day meeting of all

workers at an off-site location, described the needs for productivity improvements and reductions in costs, and put in
motion a major effort to improve the cost performance of
the plant. The company and union representatives joined
forces in using the problemsolving processes and work teams
to involve all employees in the plant in the search for solutions to problems. Thus, in this plant all of the workers have
been exposed to the LMPT concept and to a more far-
reaching cost improvement program. This accounts for the
high percentage of workers who support the process in this
plant.

Among the other five plants where interviews were conducted, only one union representative estimated that more
than 50 percent of the rank and file workers support the effort. Clearly, the local and national union representatives
face an important education and advocacy role in diffusing
worker participation through these plants.

On the other hand, interview data collected between one
and two years into these programs also indicated that support among union stewards and executive board members
generally increased over time. In three out of six plants, 100
percent of these union officers supported the process. In
another plant, 90 percent (all but one) of the local representatives supported the program. In only one plant was there as
much as a 50-50 split within the executive board over the program.

While the support of the rank and file depended on their
exposure to the process and the union officer support grew
over time, virtually all union representatives believed that
first-line supervisors and middle managers continued to
resist the process. For example, one union president stated:

> They [supervisors] are *the* problem. They are not
> educated by top management. Management has no
> means of communicating with their foremen. The
> foremen will go along with the program but they

will do it only because they have to. On the other hand, those who are now in it like it. It makes them look good and they have less to do such as less discipline and fewer grievances.

This same union president had even stronger comments about the problems with middle managers above the first-level supervisors.

They are the lost people. There is no communications there. The general foreman is trapped. He is under the most pressure for production and has to both make decisions of his own and implement the decisions of higher management of which he is often not a part. This is why they are such a difficult group to deal with and have not bought into the idea of the program yet.

In most plants it appears that the labor relations managers were also initially threatened by the program. The participation process required changes in their role and often was viewed as a threat to their own security. These managers were being asked to discard their long standing roles as the front-line adversaries protecting the firm against union encroachments on management rights. For example, a union representative described the reactions of the labor relations people in one plant as follows:

In those zones where the program (LMPTs] exists the labor relations staff have trouble justifying their existence so they don't like it. Each zone in our plant has a labor relations administrator whose central job is to manage grievances. As the LMPT program goes on, these grievance and discipline problems go away and therefore these people have less to do. The company has tried to use these people in other ways but they still fear for their own job security.

Just as the management labor relations representatives may see the program as a threat to their job security, union stewards or grievance committee representatives can also see this process as a threat to their political positions within the union. The union in one plant handled this problem by establishing an advisory committee made up of the grievance committeemen and the departmental foremen. This innovation appeared to work quite well in getting the grievance committeemen and the foremen involved in and committed to the LMPT process. It also served the "watchdog" function of resolving any jurisdictional problems that arose between the LMPT process and the grievance procedure and day-to-day contract administration.

Diffusion of the Process Through the Plant

The slow diffusion process reflects the need to first gain the commitment of the various interest groups, the need to provide adequate training to workers and supervisors before they establish their work teams, and the need to provide time and resources to the union and management facilitators, trainers, and internal and external consultants. In none of the programs of these six plants had more than one-third of the bargaining unit members been participating in work teams at the time of our interviews (approximately one-and-one-half years into the LMPT process). The percentage of bargaining unit members actually participating ranged from less than 10 percent in three plants to 33 percent in one plant. These data reinforce a conclusion that cannot be overemphasized, namely, that for worker participation efforts to survive and endure over time, there must be a strong and steady commitment to their development and evolution, and all parties involved must take a long term time perspective from the outset. Results come slowly because the process moves through these plants at a relatively slow pace.

Obstacles to Continuity

Internal Union Politics. Perhaps the obstacle to continuity in worker participation programs that has received the greatest degree of attention in the literature is the fear that worker participation processes will lead to political opposition within the local union and threaten the security of the union leadership. Ironically, this turned out to be the *least* significant threat to program continuity, not only in these six USW locals, but also in every other case we examined in this research. In only two out of the six locals did the LMPT process become an issue in the election of union officers after the process had been underway.

In one of these two locals, the candidate opposing the union president who had helped initiate the LMPT program campaigned against the process. The result was that the incumbent union president won by a stronger margin (3 to 1) than he had in his initial union election. Indeed, he reported (and it was confirmed by international union representatives) that this was the first time an incumbent president had been reelected in this local union in over 20 years. In the second case, where the issue became part of the internal union political election process, the results were more complex. The union president was reelected but believed his support for the program hurt him somewhat, especially in those areas of the plants where workers had not yet been exposed to the LMPT process. On the other hand, a number of people on the executive board who opposed the LMPT process were defeated. He described this process as follows:

> After the program got started and we began to approach the time for union elections several members of the executive board began to get nervous about their political support for the program and began to back away from it. However, those who did drop their support for it were defeated in the election.

Perhaps the best summary of the effects the LMPT process and other worker participation efforts had on internal union politics is that they can and sometimes do become an issue, but have not proven to be a determining factor in the union elections studied. Nor have internal union politics served as a serious threat to the continuity of the program in the cases studied in this research.

Layoffs. All of the plants in the steel industry have been experiencing employment cutbacks during the period in which the LMPT process was getting started. While the union representatives indicated in five out of six of these plants that the layoffs were posing some problem, in only one plant did the layoffs seriously erode support for the process. The dynamics of this particular layoff process and its impact in that plant are worth describing in some detail since they illustrate the severe threat that employment cutbacks can pose to a worker participation program.

The union representative responsible for developing the LMPT process in this plant summarized the situation as follows:

> The QWL process in this plant is dead in the water. We had a large layoff in November and our members thought that was when the QWL process should have helped but it didn't. Management called it off without any discussion. They laid off the management coordinator of QWL and the facilitator but kept all of the other vice presidents, managers, and superintendents. Our union officers feel that the majority of upper management wasn't as supportive of the program as we thought. Now the union officers aren't interested in starting it back up again even though the vice president of industrial relations wants to get it going again.

This case illustrates the important difference that a management commitment to maintain the program through hard times can make. In this plant, management's commitment did not withstand the severe market pressures experienced by the firm. This, in turn, reduced the trust and support of union officers who were then viewed as being "less than supportive" by the managers. Management then decided to set the program aside. Later, management slowly tried to rebuild support for the program but faced opposition from union officers. Their only hope then was to appeal to the job security interests of the workers. In addition, because upper management failed to maintain the principles of consultation and problemsolving in dealing with supervisors during the cutbacks, similar opposition arose towards the program from people at this level of their organization.

In the other five plants studied, although employment reductions occurred, their net effect was to slow the growth of the LMPT process rather than seriously threaten its existence.

Industry Level Negotiations. Another challenge encountered by the LMPTs was the process of negotiating a new collective bargaining agreement. Nineteen eighty-two was a year of widespread concessions in negotiations in other industries. Because of the depressed state of the steel industry, the steel companies requested an early opening of negotiations over the 1983 contract and proposed significant wage reductions. The first effort to negotiate a new agreement took place in the summer of 1982 and received a lot of public visibility and press coverage. The process broke down, however, after the chief union negotiators took a tentative agreement calling for wage cuts back to the Wage Policy Committee, a council of local union presidents which soundly rejected that agreement. Several of the local union representatives commented on the effects that experience had on the LMPTs in their plants. For example, one president stated:

> If we had just been starting up, [LMPT process] that [the negotiations] would have killed it. The im-

pression was going around the plant that, here we have this program and it is just here to help the company get concessions. But we addressed this concern directly by talking to our local people and have overcome that impression. It will [the company's strong approach in negotiations] have a bad effect.

Another local president stated:

We will survive the effects of the climate set up by these negotiations but if it continues I don't know how much longer workers will be willing to continue to be involved in the LMPTs. If we had taken the industry offer to a vote in our plant it might have turned some people who were for our LMPT program against it.

Both of these union representatives, as well as the other local leaders, stressed that it was as much *the way* in which the company approached the negotiations process as the substance of the concession proposals that bothered them. Union leaders stated that their members would accept some concessions, particularly if the concessions were tied to a commitment to reinvest funds in the steel industry. For example, a representative of a local from the U.S. Steel Company described the mood of the membership as follows:

There are two basic reasons why we won't agree. If U.S. Steel were willing to sign on the line for deferrals and that all of the money that they were saving would go back into these plants we would do that. We also believe that management is excessive in these plants given all of the layoffs that have occurred. The members do not want to give up more concessions only to see U.S. Steel use our money to purchase another big oil company.

Prior to a third effort in negotiating a new national agreement, the USW held a Wage Policy Committee meeting to outline its goals and objectives for the negotiations with the Basic Steel Industry and with other employers in steel and other industries. It decided to prepare two separate Wage Policy Committee recommendations. One set of objectives covered "distressed" industries including Basic Steel, while another set was drafted for industries in better states of health. The Wage Policy Committee report for the distressed industries included a statement outlining the union's objectives for strengthening the LMPT process. That statement is provided below.

> The Labor-Management participation team experiment in the Steel industry has proven invaluable to both parties whenever it has been tested. Armed with these results, we are determined to expand and strengthen this program which provides workers with a voice in shop-floor decisions—even those decisions once deemed to be the exclusive prerogative of management. The program should be installed in additional steel plants and introduced into other industries, but only with local union agreement. Workplace Democracy is the way of the future.

The final contract agreed to by the union and the company did include a revision of the basic language on LMPTs that strengthens the program in many of the ways proposed by the Wage Policy Committee. The major changes in the contract language can be summarized as follows.

(1) The words "joint efforts" were inserted as substitutes for "cooperative efforts" at several points in the provision. This reflected the recognition that the worker participation process is more than a cooperative process but one that involves a variety of processes, in search of solutions that meet the parties' needs.

(2) The agreement was changed from an experimental program to a basic part of the permanent relationship. That is, the intent of the changes in the language

was to take the program out of the experimental stage and make it an ongoing permanent part of the bargaining relationship.

(3)   The language was changed to provide that any local union could have an LMPT process if it so requested. This put the initiative for the program in the hands of the local union as opposed to the prior agreement which required more joint agreement to start a program between the company and the union leaders.

(4)   A new body of international union representatives and company representatives was established to oversee the development of the LMPT process and promote its diffusion to additional sites.

As a result of the industry level contract negotiations, a number of local unions have requested that international union officers begin to help them develop an LMPT program in their plants. Thus, it appears that the participation program has withstood the negotiation of a successor agreement, a farther step has been taken toward building the experimental program into the ongoing relationship, and LMPTs are likely to spread to additional plants and local unions during the term of this second agreement.

Company Level Negotiations. Although the LMPT process survived the industry level negotiations, conflicts between the U.S. Steel Corporation and the USW at both the national and local union levels have produced a crisis which led to at least a temporary and perhaps a permanent withdrawal of local union support for the LMPT process. The conflict with national union officials developed over the company's announcement that it planned to curtail production, purchase foreign steel, and maintain only the finishing portion of the steelmaking operations in one of its major plants. The union saw this shift in strategy as a breach of faith in that the announcement came shortly after the signing of the concession agreement in which union members accepted a pay cut in return for a promise that the money saved would be reinvested in steel plants. Thus, this union-company dispute was a disagreement over the linkage the union thought it had achieved between the collective bargaining agreement and the employer's basic business strategy.

Conflict also arose in a U.S. Steel plant over a local work rules dispute. Following the signing of the industry-wide contract, management proposed to the local union that a number of key job classifications be consolidated. When the local union rejected this proposal, the company began making the changes unilaterally and thus precipitated a major conflict with local union leaders. The local union leadership took the position that any changes in the organization of jobs should be discussed within existing LMPTs or through collective bargaining. Since the unilateral management actions were viewed as an act of bad faith, the local union executive board announced it would not participate in any LMPT activities unless this crisis was successfully resolved. At the time of this writing, the conflict had not been resolved and, therefore, the LMPT process was suspended. Whether it is only a temporary or a permanent breakdown of the process in this plant remains to be seen.

This breakdown illustrates the difficulty of maintaining a cooperative worker participation process in the context of fundamental union-company conflicts over basic business strategies. What makes the LMPT process especially vulnerable to these conflicts is that there is generally a low level of trust between this firm and the union. Furthermore, the company is known to prefer a traditional arms-length relationship with the union and to have a relatively weak commitment to the LMPT process.

In contrast, in one plant of a different corporation, the worker participation process expanded beyond its original intent and successfully addressed work rule issues as part of a major effort by the company and the union to attack their cost problems. A summary of this joint effort is presented below.

Early in 1982, this company began to lose significant amounts of money. The company and the union representatives had both believed that it would take about five years before the LMPTs would develop to the point where they would be paying off, so that more direct action was necessary to address the financial losses. They therefore agreed to use the basic philosophy and approach underlying the LMPT, namely, discussing the problems of the plant directly with the workers.

A team of approximately 70 people was formed to try to decide what to do. This team in turn recommended they take the problem to the entire plant population. The president agreed to shut the plant down for one full day, rented a large auditorium, and invited all employees to the meeting. At the meeting, the president, the plant manager and the industrial relations manager, outlined the cost, profit, and competitive restrictions facing the plant. The workforce was then divided into groups of about 50 to 60 people. Workers who had been trained as leaders of teams under the LMPT program led the sessions in group problemsolving and brainstorming. About 3,000 suggestions came out of these sessions and were later reduced to approximately 900 ideas. Between May and August of 1982 the implementation of these suggestions was estimated to have saved the company approximately $13 million. This was a result of an investment of approximately $250,000 (the cost of shutting the mill down for one day and paying the workers for the time at the plant meeting). The company and the union hoped to save approximately $26 million by the end of the year by implementing additional suggestions on their list.

The president of the local indicated that this strategy was successful in making that mill the low-cost producer within the company. In fact, it was getting some work that had previously gone to other mills. Finally, the union president summarized his view of where the LMPT program was leading.

We always told management that we could run the plant and they are now essentially giving us a chance to show that we can. If we are successful in doing so there will be fewer management people around in the future. We have already seen this happen since they just combined two of the general foremen's jobs into one by not replacing someone who had retired.

Summary

The experiences of the USW and the steel industry illustrate the various obstacles to continuity which arise as participation programs move through changes in the business cycle, the internal political processes within local unions and management organizations, and contract negotiations. Yet the majority of these programs (four out of the six examined here) survived. In the absence of strong local and national union support, the programs are likely to fail. Also, the absence of strong management commitment to the worker participation process, the absence of a high-trust relationship between the company and the union, or the unwillingness of management to adopt a business or industrial relations strategy that is compatible with labor-management cooperation will kill the programs. In these cases the participation process is likely to succumb to the polemics often associated with hard negotiations during formal contract renewal discussions. This apparently was the fate of the LMPT process at the U.S. Steel Corporation.

It is clear that, over time, it becomes increasingly difficult to completely separate out the LMPT process or any other worker participation program from the larger collective bargaining relationship. The strongest supporters of worker participation at the local level escalate their interest in problemsolving activities, and see grave inconsistencies between the problemsolving behaviors they have learned to use and the adversarial strategies and tactics traditionally used by unions and employers to negotiate new labor agreements.

They also see inconsistencies between the open sharing of information and consultation processes and traditional management practices in responding to economic pressures and short term crises. Finally, the statements of the local union leaders further suggest that experience with worker participation in its very narrowest sense may lead to an escalation of interest in involvement in decisionmaking on broader issues. Perhaps the best way to illustrate this point is with a statement made by one of the union presidents in summarizing his views of the process.

> I would like to think we will get more involved in bigger issues over time. We are satisfied with the involvement we have now but as the program grows our input should also grow. We should become more involved in the running of the plant if only no more than in an advisory role.

The UAW and the Automobile Industry

The auto industry's experimentation with worker participation programs began in the early 1970s. The well-publicized strike at General Motors' Lordstown plant in 1972 led to wide-ranging discussions in and out of the industry concerning the workplace environment, worker motivation, and potential avenues by which work might be reorganized and enriched.

In 1973, a letter of understanding was added to the GM-UAW national agreement recognizing

> . . . the desirability of mutual effort to improve the quality of work life for the employees. In consultation with union representatives, certain projects have been undertaken by management in the field of organizational development, involving the participation of represented employees. These and other projects and experiments which may be

undertaken in the future are designed to improve the quality of work life thereby advantaging the worker by making work a more satisfying experience, advantaging the Corporation by leading to a reduction in employee absenteeism and turnover, and advantaging the consumer through improvement in the quality of the products manufactured.

A joint national committee was created to review and encourage the QWL projects.

A variety of experimental projects followed. Among these projects was a program to enhance communication between workers and managers accompanied by a survey of worker attitudes which showed signs of early success at the GM-Lakewood assembly plant. At a van assembly plant in Detroit, assembly line operations in one work station were replaced by a team (stall) work organization. Later, the QWL program at the GM-Tarrytown assembly plant was heralded as successfully reducing absentee rates and grievance rates, and improving worker attitudes.

The pace and extent of these experimental programs varied widely within companies and across the industry. At Ford, the development of such programs stalled after a few unsuccessful pilot projects and was not revived until the end of the decade. Meanwhile, at Chrysler and American Motors, very few participation projects have been initiated. At GM, where the widest diversity of programs emerged under the leadership of Irving Bluestone of the UAW, there were failures as well as successes. For example, the team organization at the van assembly plant mentioned above failed to reach performance expectations and soon ended. The new cooperative relationship at the Lakewood assembly plant lasted only for a few years and then evaporated when plant management changed.

In some other GM plants, such as Tarrytown, there apparently are continuing successes. In the early and mid-1970s, GM also was experimenting with new work systems and managerial styles in their southern plants, most of which remained nonunion until the late 1970s. In a few of these plants workers were organized into "operating teams" with a single job classification for production workers (excluding tradesmen) and a "pay for knowledge" wage system which contained six pay levels. One of these facilities, the Delco-Remy plant in Albany, Georgia was organized by the UAW, but continued to use the team concept with the union's approval. After GM management's adoption of a neutrality pledge in 1976 and an automatic recognition clause in 1979, all of the nonunion southern plants were organized by the UAW. The development of the operating team concept, however, has had lasting effects as the use of such teams spread in the late 1970s to GM plants. This team system also is significant because, as discussed in more detail below, the system integrates basic changes in work organization and collective bargaining with worker participation.

The late 1970s witnessed a sharp economic decline in the auto industry which precipitated the development of a second generation and wider range of worker participation programs. The scale of the industry's economic decline has been massive. The employment of production workers in the industry has dropped from a peak of 802,800 in December 1978 to 511,500 as of July 1982. Furthermore, shifts in the demand for autos, heightened international competition, and the resulting imperative for rapid technological change suggest that employment levels are unlikely to return to anywhere near their earlier peaks. In addition, the enormous success of the Japanese production system raised doubts about the soundness of American labor relations practices and helped to induce a new wave of experimentation.

The economic troubles in the industry after 1979 led to significant changes in the conduct of labor-management relations. These changes include the initiation of Quality Circles at the shop floor level, and enhanced communication between workers and management through other less formal channels. To preserve jobs, a number of plants have modified local agreements and work rule practices. In the process, the role of union officers has changed dramatically. Union officials in many plants now communicate frequently with management outside of normal collective bargaining channels and receive information regarding business plans, new technologies, and supplier relations information on subjects that heretofore were deemed to be exclusive managerial prerogatives.

At Ford, worker participation programs had largely disappeared until 1980 and were encouraged by the appointment of Donald Ephlin as the vice-president of the Ford-UAW department and Peter Pestillo as the Ford vice-president of industrial relations. A further push for participation programs came in the national agreements at GM and Ford signed in 1982 which created new training programs, guaranteed income stream benefits, pilot employment guarantee projects, plant closing moratoriums, and outsourcing limitations. These agreements also included significant pay concessions (the removal of the annual improvement factor and deferral of COLA payments) and reduced the number of paid holidays by 10 per year.

The elaboration of worker participation programs in the early 1980s in the auto industry confronted two central issues. First, economic pressure clearly was a major force which spurred these programs and raised the issue of how participation programs were to relate to other cost cutting measures adopted in response to this economic pressure. Second, labor and management faced a decision regarding whether or not participation programs were to expand to the point that they entailed a more systematic transformation in industrial relations. The operating team concept adopted in a few plants provides one potential route by which this type of transformation can occur. The question is whether plants that so far have adopted more piecemeal participation programs can and will choose to move to this sort of full scale revision in the conduct of labor-management relations. To illustrate the dynamics of the participation process and the emergence of these issues, in the next section we describe events within one plant that has adopted both Quality Circles and a major work rule concessionary agreement. Then, the experiences of plants which utilize operating teams are reviewed.

A Piecemeal Participation Process

Participation programs began in this plant in 1980 in the aftermath of enormous layoffs and the emergence of doubts regarding the long term viability of the plant. This plant manufactures parts for the Ford Motor Company. Employment peaked in 1979 at 3400 hourly workers and by 1982 had fallen to 1400. Labor relations in the plant always had been, in the words of the bargaining chairman, "extremely adversarial." Facing layoffs and frustrated by their acrimonious relationship, labor and management set out in early 1980 to experiment with a worker participation process. The local union shortly discovered that language encouraging such programs had been included in their company's 1979 national agreement. Following the guidelines of the national agreement, and with advice and encouragement provided by national UAW officers, labor and management then embarked on a new program.

The participation program initially centered around the creation of "Employee Involvement" (EI) groups, essentially Quality Circles, where workers on a voluntary basis would meet for one hour a week (on paid time) and discuss workplace issues. These groups, as of the spring of 1983, included 20 percent of the hourly workforce. Expansion of EI groups has been limited by two factors—the disruptive influence of continuing layoffs and the large resources needed for group start-up. Specific issues that have been addressed by the EI groups include: the placement of a conveyor belt, the improvement of gauging operations, better lighting and the rearrangement of some work stations to better coordinate work.

The local union has made sure that contractual issues are not discussed in the EI groups. If issues such as job jurisdiction or production standards come up, discussion is "halted by the union committeeman" and the issue is sent to the plant's bargaining committee. However, in some departments, workers have become involved in broader workplace issues. A few involvement groups have been in touch with vendors to resolve production problems. Another involvement group performed a feasibility study of the use of a robot and in the process altered the ultimate decision reached by the engineering staff.

On a separate track, the relationship between union officers and plant management was changing in the plant. Union officers were being provided with information regarding business plans. For the first time, the plant manager was forewarning union officials about upcoming layoffs and new machinery, and asking for advice regarding how these changes might best be implemented. Some of their discussions have occurred as part of "Mutual Growth Forums" which follow the guidelines outlined in the 1982 national Ford-UAW agreement. Other discussions occur on a more informal basis.

An important part of the communication between plant and union officials concerned the competitive pressures faced by the plant and steps that might be taken to lower in-house production costs so as to compete more successfully for new business. These discussions led to a local agreement in 1982 which modified a number of work rules. The contractual modifications included agreements to: increase production standards; have production workers perform some housekeeping, inspection and incidental maintenance job functions; alter overtime and shift preference arrangements; and allow production workers to assist tradesmen in the repair of machines. These concessions were provided by the union on the grounds that they would lead to the arrival of new business (the plant would become a parts source for Ford's new models). In the work areas involved in any new business, it also was agreed that workers would be selected (transferred) with some consideration of ability rather than rely exclusively on existing contractual seniority provisions.

In one work area in the plant where new business has been brought in, a single ("universal") classification system has been adopted. The original plan was to include a "pay for knowledge" system in this area, though so far implementation issues have postponed that step. Management hopes that positive experience with the single classification system will encourage the system's expansion to other work areas. Expansion of this system to the whole plant essentially would amount to introduction of the operating team system.

Discussion in this plant recently has focused on shifting the Employee Involvement groups to a department team basis. Like the use of a single classification system, this shift entails a fundamental redirection of the participation process. At the core, the issue is how the participation process can be linked more closely to work rule issues, and thereby, to many of the rules currently resolved through collective bargaining procedures. From management's side, the need to more closely integrate participation and work rule issues arises from their concern that the participation process not only address "housekeeping issues," but rather focus on the problems that affect this plant's competitive position.

To date, work rule issues and the Employee Involvement process (the Quality Circles) have been procedurally kept apart. This has created two central problems. By not focusing on work rules, the agenda within the Employee Involvement groups has been limited to the point that some employees and management have become disillusioned with the outputs of the process. Furthermore, insecurities have been created within the workforce. Employees are hesitant to give up the traditional classification system and experiment with a universal classification system or other work rule changes because the job specifications and seniority rights embedded in the traditional system provide the workers with protection from the abuse of discretion by managers. If this security and protection is given up, the workers want something to be put in its place. As we will see in the later discussion of the operating team system, there it is enhanced information and participation through team structures that partially satisfies these needs.

In this plant, union officials have acquired more information and input into business decisions. Yet, this has occurred in a disassociated manner from other programs in the plant and, perhaps most important, has not fully involved the hourly workforce. Thus, although enormous change has occurred within the plant, a series of problems exist which jeopardize the future of the participation process. First, both workers and managers complain that many of the Employee Involvement groups seem to have plateaued and need to be invigorated. Second, the pace at which work rule changes have been adopted and classification systems revised has slowed due to the resistance of some work groups. Third, debilitating problems, such as whether participation in the new department teams or a new statistical quality control program are voluntary (as with the Employee Involvement groups), have slowed the adoption of these programs. Additionally, there is a sense of unease within both union and management ranks concerning where the participation process is headed and how it relates to the economic pressures confronting the plant.

To allay some of the anxieties which surfaced regarding the participation programs, a plant-wide meeting was held which involved the participation of the hourly workforce, corporate management, and national officers of the UAW. One purpose of this meeting was to show workers that the participation programs had the support of the national union. The meeting also provided the opportunity to point out the relationships between this plant's particular programs and the novel programs adopted at the national level in the 1982 negotiations.

This meeting apparently did help to broaden the support within the rank and file for the participation process. However, labor and management are still left with the problem of how to institutionalize the connection between the participation process and mainstream collective bargaining issues and procedures. The operating team system described below sets out one possible solution.

The Operating Team System

Operating teams are now utilized in 10 GM plants including the Delco-Remy plant in Albany, Georgia, Cadillac engine plant in Livonia, Michigan, and Buick 81 plant in Flint, Michigan. These plants provide an example of how the participation process can be integrated more fully with other industrial relations systems and processes.

The core of the operating team system is the departmental teams which contain a single production classification. A worker's pay thereby no longer is explicitly linked to a particular set of job tasks. Instead, there exist six pay levels which workers move up as they master a wider variety of job tasks. The work team also has responsibility for such things as inspection, material handling, housekeeping and repairs. In this way, the system involves an expansion of job tasks.

There is a "team coordinator" who functions as supervisor of the team (the former first-line supervisor's role) and an assistant team coordinator (an hourly worker). The teams regularly meet to discuss production problems, review the pay system, and discuss impending business decisions such as the introduction of new machinery or upcoming work schedules. Part of the function of team meetings is to establish a business focus within the work area. To accomplish this the team regularly reviews the costs and revenues associated with the work area. In one team meeting we observed the team coordinator reviewing the purchase vouchers accumulated by the work area in the previous week and comparing the total operating costs to operating revenues generated by the work area.

Two aspects of the typical start-up of the team systems were particularly important in providing the local union with assurances regarding management's objectives. Representatives from the local union were involved in the planning committees that shape the design and implementation of each team system. Furthermore, local union officials had a say in the initial selection of the team coordinators and continue to maintain involvement in the placement of supervisory staff.

One of the values of the single classification is that it allows greater flexibility and coordination across work stations. For instance, absenteeism is less of a problem since workers are qualified to carry out a variety of jobs. The "pay for knowledge" system reinforces this flexibility by providing a direct reward for the mastering of a large number of jobs. The work teams also allow job rotation and worker input into job design. Although these forms of work reorganization have occurred, observation of some of these plants suggests that the abandonment of assembly line techniques has not been a frequent product of the teams' operation. For one thing, the basic technologies within these plants are traditional, though being of recent vintage, and they do tend to involve a high degree of computer control. In addition, it does not appear that workers within the teams have chosen to shift away from short cycle jobs, even where they could have.

What the teams do provide is a process which links the modification of work rules and work organization to worker participation. Consider how some of the problems, which have arisen in the plant engaged in a piecemeal participation process described earlier, are resolved in the operating team system. In the piecemeal plant, participation workers are reluctant to agree to further work rule concessions for fear that the relaxation of the traditional classification and seniority system would pass too much unregulated control to management. Yet, in the operating teams it is the fact that workers receive information about upcoming changes and have a right to make their influence felt in the team meetings that provides a substitute for the security relinquished through abandonment of the traditional classification system. Furthermore, local union officials within the operating team plants receive extensive information from plant management regarding business plans. In this respect, the roles of the local union are much the same in the two plants. The difference is that in the team plants this exchange of information extends down to the level of hourly workers and is institutionalized through the team meetings.

This is not to say that all conflicts have evaporated in the team plants. One of the team plants we visited has confronted the following problems. A dispute arose over the varying pace at which workers had progressed up the levels of the "pay for knowledge" scheme across the teams. Some workers resented the fact that pay progression had been faster in an area of the plant that holds low status and in the past was a department that workers had bid out of upon accumulating seniority. This has led plant management to closely monitor and somewhat standardize pay progression across the teams. Another more serious problem exists in this plant as a consequence of the suspicion with which skilled tradesmen view the team system. In fact, a year after the start-up of teams, the skilled trades in the plant campaigned hard to have the "pay for knowledge" system (which applies only to production workers) removed. An election followed in which 65 percent of the total plant workforce voted to retain the "pay for knowledge" system. However, management has not been as successful as they initially had hoped in getting tradesmen to participate in the team system. Tradesmen apparently believe that the job-broadening and flexibility inherent in the team system ultimately threaten the identity of their crafts.

Yet, the use of teams has accomplished the removal of any artificial separation between work rule issues and participation processes. This has facilitated the creation of bargains that cut across the various issues, and thereby, allowed the kinds of compromises that are more difficult to achieve where collective bargaining and worker participation programs are kept separate.

Summary and Conclusions

The steel and auto industries have gone through their most serious economic crisis since the Great Depression. It is not surprising, therefore, that each of the worker participation processes described in this chapter has been under pressure to contribute to the economic recovery of their plants and firms. This has led the parties to search for ways of reorganizing work, improving product quality, and improving productivity. While none of the parties would agree that the primary focus of their participation efforts is to improve productivity, neither would any of the union or management representatives involved deny that improved productivity and lower operating costs are valued outcomes of their efforts.

If productivity and costs are part of the agenda, then employment security is bound to be an equally central agenda item. When participation processes begin to address these issues, it becomes increasingly difficult to draw a clear line between worker participation and collective bargaining. Thus, as the focus of the process expands, it no longer can be treated as solely a local union or local plant management issue. National union leaders and corporate executives must get involved and must decide whether or not to adjust their collective bargaining strategies in ways that support the expansion and innovation underway within the participation process. As the contrasting experiences of U.S. Steel and Ford, and to a lesser extent General Motors, illustrate, the adjustments in strategy and practice required are substantial. Top union leaders must accept significant changes in work organization and compensation structures and increased variability within previously standardized local contracts. Top management must accept greater information sharing and must stand behind commitments to business strategies that preserve the employment base of the union. It is clear that only some top executives and union leaders are ready to accept these changes.

Chapter 4

Views of the
Rank and File

Unions are political organizations whose leaders need to be responsive to the interests of their members. Therefore, no participation process is likely to succeed over an extended period of time in the absence of rank and file support. Conversely, if rank and file interest in quality of working life issues and participation processes is strong, opposition from higher level union leaders is unlikely to deter management from developing programs that build on this interest. Thus, it is appropriate to start our analysis of views toward participation experiments by assessing the views of the rank and file. By starting at this grassroot level, we also mirror the way that QWL activities evolved—from local experiments to a broader movement of significance to national union leaders.

This chapter analyzes survey data collected from rank and file union members in five national unions involved in different types of worker participation projects. The background and dynamics of four of these cases were described in chapter 2. Our analysis of the views of union members toward participation programs and the effects of these programs on members' perceptions of their jobs and their local unions will center around the following questions:

(1) Do union members assign a high enough value or priority to QWL types of issues to warrant union support for a worker participation process?

(2) Does actual participation in a QWL program lead to even greater worker interest in gaining greater say or influence over QWL types of issues?

(3) Does actual involvement in a worker participation process lead to perceptions of greater real influence over decision areas related to QWL?

(4) Does the participation process modify workers' views of their job on the key dimensions of work that participation is expected to affect such as the amount of employee job involvement, freedom, opportunity to learn new skills, etc.? These are the dimensions of job experience most often cited as the targets of QWL strategies.

(5) Does involvement in worker participation processes influence members' assessments of the performance of their union on QWL and/or other issues?

(6) To what extent do union members not currently participating in a QWL or related process want to get involved in the experiments that are underway in their plants or offices?

The Sample

The five cases for which rank and file survey data are available are not "random" samples of the experiences of all unions and their members. They do, however, span the range of worker participation programs and employer-union relationships needed to make useful comparisons and, with appropriate caution, some limited generalizations. The cases might be viewed as "samples of convenience." That is, with the help of our advisory committee we identified local unions and employers where some form of worker participation activity was underway. We then discussed our research interests with representatives of these locals. A decision to conduct a survey of rank and file workers was then made if all of the following conditions held:

(1) Sufficient time had elapsed under the worker participation project to allow for a meaningful assessment of worker views of their experiences.

(2) Some basis existed for comparing workers who were covered or actively involved in a worker participation process with similar workers who were not covered or actively involved.

(3) Both the union and the employer representatives agreed to cooperate with a survey. This proved to be one of the decisive criteria since permission to conduct a survey was needed from multiple levels of management (industrial relations or personnel professionals, QWL coordinators, plant managers, and sometimes corporate officials), multiple levels of the unions (international representatives, local union business agents, local union presidents, local union executive boards, etc.) *and* in some cases, the joint union-management steering committees overseeing the participation processes. Each of these different groups often had valid reasons for opposing surveys. Among the most common reasons were: (a) surveys had been done in the past and workers were tired of being surveyed; (b) surveys raise expectations of workers and should not be conducted unless there was a clear action plan for following up on the results; (c) the timing of the proposed survey was problematic because internal union elections were about to be

held, layoffs were in progress, about or occur, or had just occurred, or the negotiation of a new collective bargaining agreement was about to take place; or (d) the parties belived the participation process had not advanced to the point where workers were able to evaluate their experiences.

(4)   The group added diversity to the sample. That is, we wanted to collect data on a range of different types of participation programs in a variety of different employer-union relationships.

With these characteristics of the sample selection process described, we can now turn to the five cases analyzed in this chapter. It should be noted that in each case the parties were assured we would not identify individual respondents nor use the actual names of the unions and the firms without their permission. Thus fictitious union and employer names are used to describe two of the five cases (cases 2 and 3). Only brief descriptions of the cases are provided here since four of the five are analyzed in more detail in the case studies presented in chapter 2. (The case of Freeman, Inc. is not included here since the QWL and socio-technical experiments had already ended by the time our research started.)

Case 1: Local 14B and Xerox Corporation

As described in chapter 2, this case involves a large, highly skilled, blue-collar bargaining unit located in Xerox's manufacturing complex in Rochester, New York. The union and the company began a jointly administered QWL program in late 1980 after a clause authorizing experimentation with such a program was included in their 1980 bargaining agreement. Survey data were collected from a sample of 387 out of a bargaining unit of approximately 4,000 workers. The data were collected during the summer of 1982, approximately 20 months after the start-up of the QWL project. In this case the union involved in the QWL project acts as a full joint sponsor and sits with representatives of management on all of the various steering and oversight committees. The actual participation process resembles a Quality Circle (QC) program.

Case 2: Local 2 and the Uniform Piston Company

This is a bargaining unit of approximately 300 semi-skilled and unskilled workers located in a small manufacturing plant. The structure of the participation process again resembles a QC program. In this case, the union is less centrally involved in the different stages of the process and adopts more of a "watchdog" rather than a joint sponsor role. The program had been in effect for approximately two years prior to conducting the survey in the autumn of 1982.

Case 3: Local 25 and the Communication Services Corporation

This is a large bargaining unit of blue-collar workers covering a wide range of skills employed in a facility of a large communications services firm. The QWL process in this firm is only in the early stages of development. It had been in place less than one year prior to our survey in late 1982. For this reason, we did not conduct a full case study of the program and therefore this case is not discussed in chapter 2. It is included here, however, because it provided data on a sample of workers in the early stages of a QWL process. The process is part of a nationwide program that has been underway since the signing of a national agreement in 1980 in which the union and the company agreed to jointly develop a QWL program in its various locations. The union and management serve as joint sponsors of the process which also is similar to a QC program.

Case 4: Local 717 and Packard Electric

This is a large bargaining unit of approximately 9,000 workers represented by Local 717 of the IUE employed by

Packard Electric, a division of General Motors Corporation. Data were collected from 104 workers in various adjacent plants of a large manufacturing complex located in Warren, Ohio. This case serves as our longest running QWL process in the sample. Discussions of joint activities between the union and the firm date back to 1977 and formal QWL activities have been underway since 1978. In addition, this case provides data from union members in a QWL process that has gone beyond the QC stage by experimenting with autonomous work groups and work team organizations. The local union has been a full joint partner in developing and administering the participation activities since 1977.

Case 5: The Newspaper Guild and the Minneapolis and St. Paul Newspaper

These data are collected from two units in the same local of the Newspaper Guild (NG) located in Minneapolis and St. Paul, Minnesota. The Minneapolis unit is covered by the labor-management committee called the Worker Participation Committee (WPC) described in chapter 2. The WPC grew out of a 1972 collective bargaining agreement. It is a joint union-management committee that discusses a wide range of topics including working conditions, new technology, systems for performance appraisal, the selection of assistant editors, etc. The St. Paul unit of the NG does not have a labor-management committee in place and therefore provides a comparison group of comparable workers not covered by a labor-management committee. This case provides both a different type of participation structure (a labor-management committee as opposed to direct involvement of individuals and small work teams) and a white-collar professional employee group as opposed to blue-collar manufacturing or service workers. Because this unit and its participation program differ in these ways from the others, it will be treated separately in much of the statistical analysis that follows and will not be included in the regression analyses which combine the data from the other four cases.

Research Design Considerations

Obviously, the ideal way to assess the effects of participation processes on a set of workers would be to collect data on their views of their work and their union prior to the start of the process and then collect follow-up data at some appropriate point after the process has been in effect. That was not possible given the time and resource constraints of this study. Instead, we took advantage of the variation in exposure to these processes within each organization by comparing the views of workers participating in the processes with the views of workers who were not involved at the time of our survey. Regression analysis was then used to control for other differences in the characteristics of the workers that might be correlated with their assessments of their jobs and their union. The key results of the regressions are reported in the text. The specific coefficients are reported in an appendix to the chapter.

Our preference was to collect the survey data from the parties directly as part of our case study process. This was possible to arrange in three of the five cases (cases 1, 2, and 4). Surveys were administered to small groups of workers at the workplace on company time by a member of our research team. In cases 3 and 5, however, we needed to collect the data by mail survey since the employees were too dispersed to make the collection of data in small groups of workers feasible. The response rate for the mail surveys was 38 percent in case 3 and 40 percent in case 5. In both cases the proportions of participants and nonparticipants who responded mirrored the actual proportions in these two groups in the larger bargaining unit. Analysis of the distributions of the data across the cases showed no systematic differences due to the nature of the data collection method used.

Demographic Characteristics

Table 4-1 provides a demographic profile of the pooled sample of union members included in these cases. Overall, survey data are available from approximately 931 workers of whom approximately 446 are currently participating in or covered by a worker participation process and 485 are non-participants. The exact sample size varies in the analyses reported below because of missing data on some of the questions.

The average worker in the sample is 39 years old, earns approximately $11.80 per hour and has 13 years of seniority with his or her employer. Thirty-one percent of the sample is female and 13 percent are members of a minority group. Six percent of the sample have less than a high school education, 95 percent completed high school, 29 percent have some college or post high school experience, and 20 percent have a college degree. As the data in table 4-1 indicate, there are few significant differences in the characteristics of the participants and nonparticipants. Participants have, on average, two years more seniority with the company and are less likely to be members of a minority group than are nonparticipants. Although these average differences appear to be relatively insignificant, in the analyses to follow we will control for variations in these characteristics as we attempt to estimate the net effects of these worker participation processes.

Participants, on average, have a history of being slightly more active in union affairs than nonparticipants. These differences are also highlighted in table 4-1. For example, participants were more likely to be members of union committees, have attended union meetings, and voted in union elections. While these are not large differences, they do indicate that those who get involved in worker participation processes tend to be the same individuals who have higher than average rates of participation in union affairs. We control for degree of prior union participation in the regression results reported

Table 4-1
Demographic Profile

	Total sample	Participants	Nonparticipants
	N = 931	N = 446	N = 485
Age (Years)	39.3	39.2	39.3
Sex (% Female)	30.7	28.2	33.1
Race (% Nonwhite)	12.3	10.4	14.0
Education (% High school or beyond)	94.5	94.4	94.6
Company seniority (Years)	12.5	11.7*	13.3*
Hourly wage rate ($/hour)	11.80	12.20	11.50
Union steward (%)	3.5	4.1	3.0
Member of a union committee (%)	6.2	9.7***	3.0***
Member of union executive board (%)	3.0	3.1	2.8
Local union officer (%)	1.8	1.2	2.4
Attended a meeting in last year (%)	48.2	54.4**	42.6**
Voted in last union election (%)	85.3	90.1***	80.1***
Ran for union office (%)	6.2	7.2	5.3
Called union office in last year (%)	62.2	63.9	60.6

*Indicates a significant difference at a 10% confidence level.
**Indicates a significant difference at a 5% confidence level.
***Indicates a significant difference at a 1% confidence level.

below in order to avoid attributing any differences due to prior union involvement to the effects of involvement in a participation process.

Interest in Participation

One of the first questions union leaders must consider when deciding whether or not to support a worker participation process is whether rank and file union members are interested enough in gaining some say or influence over the issues likely to be discussed for the union and the company to embark on a participation program. More specifically, union leaders need to ask whether rank and file interest in QWL types of issues is equal to or greater than interest in the bread and butter issues that unions have traditionally emphasized in collective bargaining. In addition, union leaders must often educate their members to the importance of longer run strategic issues that may be rather distant from the consciousness of most workers, yet may affect their long run interests. Thus, in evaluating the degree of interest workers express in QWL issues, it is useful to compare the relative priorities members attach to QWL, traditional bread and butter, and longer run strategic issues generally reserved to management.

The data presented in table 4-2 allow this type of comparison for participants and nonparticipants across the five cases. To measure the importance of the QWL issues, those surveyed were asked whether they wanted "no say," "a little say," "some say" or "a lot of say" over a range of workplace issues. Table 4-2 reports the percentage of participants and nonparticipants from each case that responded they wanted "some" or "a lot" of say over QWL, bread and butter, and strategic issues.

The responses show there generally is a very high level of interest among workers in all five cases in the issues most central to QC or QWL processes. For example, between 67 percent and 96 percent of these union members want some or a lot of say over the way work is done or the methods and procedures used to perform their jobs. Similarly, between 79 percent and 96 percent want some or a lot of say over the quality of the work produced and between 67 percent and 88 percent want this much influence over the pace of work. Interest tapers off slightly in having a high degree of influence over two QWL issues that are central topics of experiments in work reorganization or autonomous work groups. That is, between 39 percent and 73 percent of the respondents report wanting some or a lot of say over how much work should be done in a day and over how jobs are assigned within a work group.

While the desire for influence over QWL issues is quite high, worker interests are not limited to this subset of issues. For example, between 64 percent and 93 percent of the respondents want some or a lot of say over the traditional bread and butter issue of wages. Similarly, approximately two-thirds to four-fifths of the respondents want to influence the handling of complaints or grievances and a similar number want to influence the strategic issues of new technology. There is, however, considerably less interest expressed by the majority of these union members in gaining say or influence over other personnel decisions that have traditionally been left to management discretion (subject to relevant provisions of the bargaining agreement) such as the hiring, firing, and promotion of bargaining unit members, the setting of management salaries, and the selection of managers. The major exception to this statement, however, is found in the responses of the professional employee group (case 5). Among this sample there is considerably more interest expressed in the issues of selection of supervisors, managers, and fellow workers and in the handling of promotions. These are all critical issues that have been discussed by the labor-management committee covering this group. It is not surprising, therefore, that the group expresses a higher level of interest in these issues.

Table 4-2
Interest in Participation by Areas of Concern
Participants and Nonparticipants

(% of respondents agreeing they want "some say" or "a lot of say")

	Case 1		Case 2		Case 3		Case 4		Case 5	
	Part's	Non-part's	Part's	Non-part's	Part's	Non-part's	Part's	Non-part's	Part's	Non-part's
	N=218	N=169	N=15	N=45	N=31	N=139	N=52	N=49	N=130	N=83
QWL Concerns										
The way the work is done—methods and procedures	87	79	67**	91**	87	92	96**	78**	96	94
The level of quality of work	85	79	80	81	94	87	92	82	96	96
How fast the work should be done—the work rate	80	68	67	71	84	81	77	76	88	81
How much work people should do in a day	59	50	47	43	63	65	64	59	72	66
Who should do what job in your group or section	52*	39*	73	51	42	53	69	56	63	57
Bread and Butter Concerns										
When the work days begin and end	52	48	33	33	74	60	62	69	77	74
Pay scales or wages	70	64	73	80	74	84	73	74	93	90
Who should be fired if they do a bad job or don't come to work	38	40	33	40	42	38	44*	25*	52***	27***

Who should be hired into your work group	39	30	20	24	29	33	42	31	52**	35**
Handling complaints or grievances	66	67	60	73	71	72	62	57	83	74
Who gets promoted	43	35	27	27	36	43	44	37	54*	40*
Strategic Concerns										
The use of new technology on your job	73*	63*	80*	67*	65	69	85	69	82	77
Management salaries	29	24	20	22	3*	15*	39	43	27**	15**
Hiring or promotions to upper management	38*	23*	7	9	23	26	27	35	52***	30***
The selection of your supervisor	50*	30*	20	18	36	40	56	47	63**	49**
Plant expansions, closings, or new locations	47	43	13	24	48	52	67	74	42	39
The way the company invests its profits or spends its money	48	44	53	51	36	42	49	38	36	27

*Indicates a significant difference at a 10% confidence level.

**Indicates a significant difference at a 5% confidence level.

***Indicates a significant difference at a 1% confidence level.

For cases 1 and 4, both blue-collar units where the local union is actively involved as a joint partner in the QWL process, there is a tendency for participants to indicate a stronger interest in having "some" or "a lot" of say over QWL issues than their comparison group of nonparticipants. The same general position, although weaker in magnitude, is present in the responses of the white-collar unit in case 5. In the other two cases, however, there are no consistent differences in interest in QWL issues across the two groups. When the average responses of participants and nonparticipants are compared as a whole across all the cases (without controlling for other characteristics), there is a statistically significant difference that indicates participants do on average have greater interest in QWL issues than nonparticipants.

Participants also indicate a stronger interest in a number of strategic issues, most notably those relating to management and supervisor hirings, promotions, salaries and the investment policies of the firm. Again these differences are more consistent in cases 1 and 5 than in cases 2 and 3.

There are at least two possible explanations for differences in the preferences observed between participants and nonparticipants. One interpretation is that those who volunteer for QWL training and team activities had a higher degree of interest in participation from the outset than those who chose not to get involved. Alternatively, one could interpret the data as suggesting that the actual experience of participating in the QWL process has increased the interest of employees in gaining some say over these issues and/or over issues traditionally left to the prerogatives of management. Undoubtedly, both of these interpretations are partially true. Indeed, further analysis of these data using a regression equation are reported in the appendix to this chapter. This regression controls for differences in demographic characteristics between participants and nonparticipants in cases 1 through 4 (the Newspaper Guild observations are excluded from these and all subsequent regressions since the structure of their program is one of a labor-management committee rather than a direct form of worker participation). The regression results show that after controlling for demographic characteristics, the amount of say and influence desired over QWL issues by participants is still higher, but not significantly higher than by nonparticipants. Similarly, after controlling for demographic differences, participants show a slightly higher degree of interest than do nonparticipants in influence over both bread and butter and strategic issues. These results imply that participation in a QWL process does marginally increase the average worker's interest in having greater say over QWL as well as over selected bread and butter and strategic issues.

The results of the analysis of worker preferences for say or influence in QWL and other issues can be summarized as follows. First, a strong majority—more than four out of five workers—want to have say over the issues typically associated with Quality Circles, namely, the way work is done and the quality of the work produced. This suggests that union efforts to address these issues are well placed. Second, those who are currently participating in a QWL process on average report a slightly higher degree of interest in QWL issues than those not currently involved in such a program. Furthermore, participants also report a somewhat stronger interest in gaining a say over several strategic managerial decisions and over those personnel and working conditions issues that most directly affect their work group. While some of these differences in preferences may be due to differences in the predispositions of participants and nonparticipants (i.e., those with a higher degree of interest in gaining a say over these issues volunteered for the programs), some of the differences between participants and nonparticipants appear to be due to involvement in QWL programs. Third, a majority of workers, regardless of whether or not they are participating in QWL activities, want some or a lot of say over the traditional bread and butter issues of wages and grievance handling. Fourth, while a majority of blue-collar workers did not express a strong interest in having a say over most of the strategic issues generally reserved to management, between two-thirds to four-fifths do want to be involved in decisions over the use of new technology on their jobs.

Amount of Actual Influence

We now turn to the question of whether workers who are currently participating in a QWL or other type of worker participation process perceive *actually* having greater say or influence over workplace issues. The data needed to answer this question are reported in table 4-3.

All workers report having considerably less actual say or influence over QWL and other issues than they prefer to have, regardless of whether or not they are currently involved in a worker participation process. Only in the case of the newspaper workers does a majority report having some or a lot of say over the way work is done and over the quality of the work performed. Only in case 4 does a larger percentage of participants consistently indicate having greater say or influence over QWL types of issues than nonparticipants. In the other cases, apparently the worker participation processes have not significantly altered the degree of actual say or influence workers experience on their jobs.

When cases 1 through 4 are combined and differences in demographic characteristics are controlled, only marginal and nonsignificant differences are found between participants and nonparticipants in the amount of actual influence. Thus, of the worker participation programs studied here, only case 4 has produced a measurable increase in the say or influence experienced by the workers involved.

Table 4-3
Perception of Actual Influence by Areas of Concern
Participants and Nonparticipants

(% of respondents agreeing they have "some say" or "a lot of say")[1]

	Case 1		Case 2		Case 3		Case 4		Case 5	
	Part's	Non-part's	Part's	Non-part's	Part's	Non-part's	Part's	Non-part's	Part's	Non-part's
QWL Concerns										
The way the work is done—methods and procedures	31	38	40	26	32	28	35	25	58	47
The level of quality of work	43	42	47	47	36	40	50	34	57	57
How fast the work should be done—the work rate	17	16	13	26	23	24	14	10	32	28
How much work people should do in a day	11	9	0	5	3	11	6	8	17	19
Who should do what job in your group or section	8	9	20	19	7	7	36***	10***	18	22
Bread and Butter Concerns										
When the work days begin and end	9	9	7	16	16	13	12	4	33*	45*
Pay scales or wages	11	13	53*	30*	10	8	12	10	54	47
Who should be fired if they do a bad job or don't come to work	3	6	7	7	0	1	4	0	8	10
Who should be hired into your work group	3	4	2	0	0	1	4	2	2	5

(continued)

Table 4-3 (continued)

	Case 1		Case 2		Case 3		Case 4		Case 5	
	Part's	Non-part's	Part's	Non-part's	Part's	Non-part's	Part's	Non-part's	Part's	Non-part's
Handling complaints or grievances	14***	22***	40	40	13	18	12	2	40	37
Who gets promoted	2	4	0	0	0	1	4	0	6	4
Strategic Concerns										
The use of new technology on your job	18	22	20	17	7	12	22	14	16	13
Management salaries	2	2	0	0	0	0	2	0	1	1
Hiring or promotions to upper management	3	2	0	0	0	0	4	0	2	1
The selection of your supervisor	4	4	0	2	0	1	6	0	7	2
Plant expansions, closings, or new locations	3	4	0	2	0	3	8	2	0	0
The way the company invests its profits or spends its money	4	4	0	0	0	4	4	0	0	0

NOTE: Sample sizes are the same as in table 4-2.

*Indicates a significant difference at a 10% confidence level.

***Indicates a significant difference at a 1% confidence level.

Views of the Job

Another way of examining the effects of worker participation processes is to determine whether participants have different perceptions of the nature of their jobs than nonparticipants. Specifically, QWL processes are often viewed as strategies for allowing workers to learn new skills, increase their freedom on the job, provide more control over the pace and content of their work, and provide more information on how their work fits into the overall production process. To assess the effects of worker participation processes on these job dimensions, those surveyed were asked the extent to which they agreed with the statements listed in table 4-4. We have reported the percentages of participants and nonparticipants who "agreed" or "strongly agreed" with each of these statements. Since these questions once again are more relevant to participation processes that involved workers directly rather than indirect forms of participation such as a labor-management committee, data from the Newspaper Guild local are not included in these analyses.

Responses to these questions in cases 1, 2, and 3 are mixed and form no consistent pattern. The participants in the QWL process in case 4, however, consistently rate their jobs more favorably than nonparticipants. It should be recalled that case 4 is the bargaining unit in which the union has been a full joint partner in major work reorganization efforts and the QWL program there goes considerably beyond the more limited programs found in the other three cases. Thus, these data suggest that those participation programs that move beyond the limited problemsolving focus of the standard QC process and directly modify the structure and layout of the organization of work are more likely to have significant effects on the workers' perceptions of the favorableness of their jobs. Since our sample provides only one case where the QWL program has evolved to this point and shows this result, the evidence on this point is only suggestive.

Table 4-4
Views of the Job by Participants and Nonparticipants
(% of respondents who "agree" or "strongly agree")[1]

	Case 1		Case 2		Case 3		Case 4		Case 5	
	Part's	Non-part's	Part's	Non-part's	Part's	Non-part's	Part's	Non-part's	Part's	Non-part's
My job requires that I keep learning new things.	77	69	87	71	94	86	75**	51**	89	92
I have the freedom to decide what I do on my job.	41	41	67	47	61	51	39**	19**	62	64
I get to do a number of different things on my job.	82	84	100**	76**	87	86	83*	65*	91	93
My job lets me use my skills and abilities.	66*	58*	60	76	71	70	45*	27*	85	86
Most of the time I know what I have to do on my job.	96	95	93*	100*	90	96	100	92	98	94
I never seem to have enough time to get everything done on my job.	38	40	33	29	48	42	23	25	48	42
I determine the speed at which I work.	65	67	93	98	61*	76*	35*	18*	59	58
It is hard to tell what impact my work makes on the product or service.	54*	44*	20	29	39	34	23***	56***	37**	23**
The work I do on my job is meaningful to me.	80	75	87	78	84	80	79***	52***	87	87

I feel personally responsible for the work I do on my job.	94	92	87	96	90	94	94*	81*	98	95
My job has rules and regulations concerning everything I might do or say.	58	57	47	56	74	68	54	53	21	17

NOTE: Sample sizes are the same as in table 4-2.

*Indicates a significant difference at a 10% confidence level.

**Indicates a significant difference at a 5% confidence level.

***Indicates a significant difference at a 1% confidence level.

When we control for demographic differences in the total sample, a significant difference between participants and nonparticipants is still observed. Part of this is undoubtedly due to the influence of the respondents from case 4, but the marginal differences seen in the other cases also contribute to this result. Thus, overall, there is some evidence that these QWL processes are improving the extent. to which workers see their jobs as challenging, offering opportunities to learn and use existing skills and abilities, and provide more freedom. The largest differences on these dimensions of workers' jobs are found in the program that goes the farthest in broadening the scope of the job and reorganizing the work to conform to more of a team organization concept.

Views of Union Performance

One of the most important and hotly debated issues within the labor movement pertains to the effects that union participation in these QWL types of programs will have on members' views of their union. Advocates of greater union involvement in worker participation programs argue that as a result, workers will see the union as more effectively representing their interests at the workplace because their job experiences are improving and union efforts are seen as an important cause of the improvement. Those who argue against union involvement in these programs, on the other hand, fear that membership support for their union will decline as a result of these participation programs, since the perceived need for a union will decline.

To address this set of issues, respondents were asked to rate the performance of their local union on a variety of QWL, bread and butter, strategic, and internal union administration issues. In addition, respondents were asked to rate their overall satisfaction with their local union. The responses of participants and nonparticipants are shown in table 4-5.

Several clear patterns emerge from these data. First, all of these local unions are given higher performance ratings on the traditional bread and butter issues than on the strategic, QWL, or internal union administration issues. For example, across the sample the five issues for which the unions are given the highest performance ratings are all bread and butter issues, namely, improving wages, improving fringe benefits, protecting members against unfair treatment, handling grievances, and improving safety and health. A strategic issue (challenging management policies) and a QWL issue (making this a better place to work) only compete with the remaining bread and butter issue (job security) for a place in the performance ranking. Further examination of the percentages rating their union on QWL issues shows that only in the case of the white-collar Newspaper Guild group and case 4, the blue-collar unit that has gone beyond the QC program to modify the organization of work, do a majority of union members rate their union as doing a "somewhat good" or "very good " job. Thus, overall, there appears to be considerable room for improvement in union performance on QWL issues.

Examination of the differences in union performance ratings between participants and nonparticipants suggests three key conclusions. First, the union in case 4 again received significantly more positive ratings from participants versus nonparticipants on all measures of union performance. No other case approaches the size and strength of the differences between participants and nonparticipants observed in this unit. For example, 85 percent of the participants in this local rate the union as doing a good or very good job in improving productivity, compared to 57 percent of the nonparticipants. Eighty-one percent of the participants give the union this rating on the issue of making their plant a better place to work, compared to 49 percent of the nonparticipants. The same pattern continues for each of the QWL, strategic, bread and butter, and internal union administra-

Table 4-5
Perceptions of Union Performance by Areas of Concern
Participants and Nonparticipants

(% of respondents rating the union as doing a "good" or "very good job")[1]

	Case 1		Case 2		Case 3		Case 4		Case 5	
	Part's	Non-part's	Part's	Non-part's	Part's	Non-part's	Part's	Non-part's	Part's	Non-part's
QWL Concerns										
Getting workers a say in how they do their jobs	39	37	33	50	32	20	62*	43*	58***	29***
Helping make jobs more interesting	20	23	7	24	13	15	58***	25***	28**	16**
Making this a better place to work	55	52	43	53	45	49	81***	49***	69	70
Helping improve productivity	40	41	27	38	30	28	85***	57***	33	23
Getting management to listen to workers' suggestions	51	52	47	32	36	32	69***	39***	77***	36***
Bread and Butter Concerns										
Protecting members against unfair treatment	80***	68***	53***	89***	55	53	87***	50***	85	84
Getting good wages	89	87	67	82	84	83	83	71	97	98
Getting good fringe benefits	87	82	67	76	81	80	77*	57*	86***	67***
Improving job security	45	45	53	67	45	41	75***	41***	82	88
Handling grievances	73*	64*	73	87	45	42	85***	49***	85	86
Improving safety and health	68	66	60	80	58	62	83***	55***	82***	42***

Strategic Concerns									
Getting workers a say in the business	30**	13	23	26	15	52***	20***	57***	16***
Representing worker interests in management decisionmaking	36	36	40	19	24	64***	33***	78***	46***
Challenging management policies that are harmful to workers' interests	59**	60	40	36	41	77***	35***	77	76
Union Administration Concerns									
Giving members a say in how the union is run	35	53	73	29*	47*	54***	25***	80	75
Telling members what the local union is doing	32	53	65	29*	45*	65*	45*	83	81
Overall Union Satisfaction									
Percent "satisfied" or "very satisfied" with the union	55	67	84	37	45	75***	31***	84	81

NOTE: Sample sizes are the same as in table 4-2.
*Indicates a significant difference at a 10% confidence level.
**Indicates a significant difference at a 5% confidence level.
***Indicates a significant difference at a 1% confidence level.

tion issues. Similarly, in response to the global question on satisfaction with the union, 75 percent of the participants indicated that they are "satisfied" or "very satisfied" with their union, compared to 31 percent of the nonparticipants. These differences remain significant even after controlling for differences in demographic characteristics between participants and nonparticipants. This provides some assurance that the differences reported in this table are not due to some factor other than the worker participation process.

Second, those Newspaper Guild members covered by the labor-management committee (case 5) rate their union higher on those QWL and strategic issues that deal with the union's ability to represent its members in management decisionmaking. For example, the largest differences between those covered by the committee and those not covered are found on the issues of: (1) getting management to listen to workers' suggestions (77 percent to 36 percent); (2) getting workers a say in the business (57 percent to 16 percent); (3) representing worker interests in management decisionmaking (78 percent to 46 percent); and (4) getting workers a say in how they do their jobs (58 percent to 29 percent). Those covered by the committee also give the union higher ratings on helping to make jobs more interesting (28 percent to 16 percent), getting good fringe benefits (86 percent to 67 percent), and improving safety and health (82 percent to 42 percent). These differences imply that a labor-management committee that is successful in engaging management in serious discussions of issues that normally lie beyond collective bargaining can enhance the effectiveness of the union in dealing with a set of strategic issues that it otherwise would have difficulty influencing.

Third, in case 1, the union also receives consistently higher ratings from those participating in the QWL program on several issues measuring the union's influence in management decisionmaking. None of these differences, however, approach the size of the differences found in case 4. Further-more, there are no significant differences in the ratings of participants and nonparticipants for this union on QWL issues. This pattern is consistent with the responses of members of the unions in case 2 and 3 as well. Thus, the role and efforts of the union in case 4 has produced a greater difference in participant versus nonparticipant ratings of union performance than the other cases.

When the data from all cases are combined and a regression equation is computed that controls for differences in demographic characteristics, we again find that, on average, participants rate union performance on QWL issues marginally, but not significantly, higher than nonparticipants.

In summary, there is no evidence in these data to support the critics' argument that the presence of a QWL program will undermine workers' support of their union. Indeed, the evidence suggests that local unions are rated as being marginally more effective by members who are involved in worker participation processes than by nonparticipants. Furthermore, the local union is rated as significantly more effective in the case of the union with the highest degree of involvement and the most advanced form of participation.

Interest in Future Participation

The final question addressed in the survey was whether nonparticipants were interested in getting involved in the worker participation process. Thirty-five percent of the nonparticipants in cases 1 through 4 indicated a desire to get involved, however wide variations existed in the response to this question across these four cases. For example, only 15 percent of the nonparticipants in case 2 indicated an interest in getting involved in the QWL program and only 25 percent expressed this interest in case 1. In contrast, 55 percent indicated an interest in getting involved in the participation program in case 4, while 63 percent indicated an interest in joining the QWL program in case 3.

What accounts for these large differences? One thing that *does not* appear to explain these differences is variation in the demographic characteristics of the respondents. A regression showed there were no significant differences in age, education, race, sex, company seniority or nature of current job between those indicating a preference for getting involved in the worker participation process in their organization and those indicating that they prefer to not get involved. Thus, it appears to be the way in which the specific programs are perceived by nonparticipants that influences their interest in joining them.

In case 1, where only 25 percent of the nonparticipants indicated an interest in joining the QWL process, evidence gathered in less structured interviews strongly suggests that worker interest in the QWL process had plateaued and begun to taper off. We noted the reasons for this in chapter 2, namely, a large number of layoffs and permanent workforce reductions were occurring in this bargaining unit. As a result, at the time of our survey the QWL process was going through a major testing period with many of its early supporters questioning its utility for making their jobs, and the jobs of their co-workers, more secure. Therefore, it is not surprising that three out of four of the nonparticipants questioned the benefits to be derived from joining the QWL process.

In case 2, where only 15 percent of the nonparticipants want to get involved, we have a similar situation where layoffs had been occurring as the firm shifted production out of the plant to a newer nonunion plant in the South. Case 2 is also a QC type of process with a limited "watchdog" role for the union. Thus, there appears to be a limited commitment from the employer to the long-run job security of the workers and the organizational security of the union. Not surprisingly, therefore, there is limited rank and file interest in joining the QC program.

Case 3 is an emerging QWL process in its first year of development. At the time of our survey only 18 percent of the bargaining unit was involved in the QWL program. However, a great deal of interest was expressed by the parties in seeing the program expand to more workers consistent with the finding that 63 percent of the nonparticipants wanted to join the QWL process.

Case 4 is our best example of a long-standing participation process with a high degree of union involvement and commitment. It also is a case in which the union has treated the participation process as part of its larger representation strategy for improving the job security of the membership and enhancing the competitiveness of the firm. It also is the case in which the data show that those currently participating rate their jobs *and* the local union more favorably than those not participating. All this helps explain why 55 percent of the nonparticipants in this organization express an interest in joining the participation process.

Summary and Conclusions

No survey data should ever stand alone. Conclusions reached from surveys are always strengthened when combined with more intensive knowledge of the context in which the data are collected. Therefore, the conclusions reported here build not only on the specific survey results, but also on the insights gained from the case studies presented in chapter 2.

In case 1, the QWL process started with a great deal of rank and file interest in the process (both among those currently involved and those not involved), but tapered off considerably as concerns for job security increased in the face of layoffs. Despite the strong presence of the union in the QWL process, neither the participants nor the nonparticipants gave the union high marks for its performance on QWL issues. Indeed, the limited QC nature of this program did not produce any perceptible improvements in the amount of say or influence on the job experienced by participants, nor did it significantly alter these workers' evaluations of their jobs. Thus, from this case we have learned the difficulty a union will experience in maintaining rank and file support for a limited QWL process in the face of deteriorating circumstances that challenge the ability of the union to effectively represent rank and file interests on traditional bread and butter issues. It also suggests that a QWL process may experience a plateauing of support and interest after the first blush of excitement and experimentation wears off. This plateauing phenomenon challenges the union and the employer to decide whether they are to recommit their organizations to enhancing the QWL process or allow it to continue to erode and eventually fade out of existence.

Case 2 illustrates the pitfalls a union may experience with a limited QC program in which it chooses to play only a "watchdog" role. The survey data in this case suggest that the union members do not see significant change in their jobs or their influence in decisionmaking and do not see the union as performing significantly better on QWL issues as a result of the program. At the same time, rank and file evaluations of union performance have not yet suffered from the QC program.

Case 3 represents a QWL process in the early stages of development. It demonstrates that QWL programs diffuse slowly through organizations and that while interest in participating is often quite strong in its initial stages, positive results from the process may not be visible in the short run.

Case 4 is an example of a participation process that has been in place for more than five years, that has moved into the area of work reorganization, and that has achieved the most positive response from rank and file workers. It suggests that the participation processes that are likely to have the most positive long-run outcomes for unions and their members are ones that become integrated into the union and the employer's broader strategies for enhancing workers' job security and the firm's economic performance.

Case 5 is different from the other cases since it includes a labor-management committee covering white-collar professional workers. The survey results for this group suggest that while the indirect participation structure of a labor-management committee is unlikely to significantly affect individual worker experiences on their job on a day-to-day basis, it can serve as a useful forum for discussing on an ongoing basis the larger strategic issues that otherwise are left to management's discretion.

When considered as a whole, these survey data suggest that worker participation processes can have a positive effect on workers' job-related experiences and on their evaluation of the performance of their union. Positive impacts, however, are slow in developing and do not stand independent from other union activities, accomplishments, or shortcomings. That is, there is no evidence in these data that a union would be strengthened by being an active and visible partner in a worker participation process in the face of poor union performance on its traditional bread and butter responsibilities. Stated differently, effective performance on QWL issues will not serve as an effective substitute for an inability to deliver economic benefits, job security and protection from any arbitrary actions on the part of management. The variations across these cases suggest that improvements in workers' views of their jobs and their unions are greater where:

(1)   the union serves as a visible joint partner in the process;

(2) the participation process leads to actual changes in work organization that enhance the security of the labor force and the economic performance of the firm;

(3) union leaders link their support for QWL to their larger collective bargaining and representational strategies, and;

(4) sufficient time has passed for the union's contribution to improving QWL experiences of their members to be seen while at the same time the union continues to effectively deal with bread and butter concerns.

Union performance on QWL issues still has considerable room for improvement. Even in cases where unions are serving as a joint partner in delivering QWL services, union performance on these issues is rated lower than performance on bread and butter issues. On average, less than a majority of union members rate their union as performing well on QWL issues, even in those cases where a QWL process is underway.

QWL programs go through various stages of development in which worker reactions to the process and to the union's role are likely to vary. Since interested workers may get involved first, there is likely to be an initial burst of enthusiasm and interest in the process prior to the participants forming a judgment about its effects on their jobs and their relationship to the union. Later, a tapering off or plateauing of enthusiasm may occur and the remaining nonparticipants are likely to resist efforts to get them involved. The ultimate degree of interest in and support for the process is likely to be determined by the extent to which the union is able to successfully use the process to both improve individual workers' direct or day-to-day job experience as well as improve the long-run security of those jobs.

While rank and file support provides the essential foundation for worker participation processes, their long-run viability also depends on the views of local and national union officers and on the ability of the parties to fit the participation process and its results into their larger bargaining relationship. In the chapters that follow we move up from the grass roots level and analyze the views of local union officers and national union leaders to better understand where participation processes fit into labor-management relations.

Appendix to Chapter 4

The table contained in this appendix reports the results of regression equations used to estimate the effects of worker participation on the workers' views of their job and their union. The numbers reported in the table are unstandardized regression coefficients for dummy variables that took the value of 1 if the worker was participating in a worker participation process and 0 if the worker was not participating. The following control variables were entered into each equation: age, race, sex, educational level, years with the firm, hourly wage rate, and an index of participation in union activities. Another set of equations was computed which contained dummy variables for each union. The conclusions discussed in the chapter are based on the more conservative results that contain the controls for differences across the local unions.

The dependent variables were calculated by first grouping the issues into (1) quality of work, (2) bread and butter, and (3) strategic categories as shown in tables 4-2, 4-3, and 4-5. Averages within group scores were then computed and serve as the dependent variables for these analyses. The dependent variable for the test of whether participation affects workers' views of their job content is the average response to all the items contained in table 4-4. The dependent variable for overall union satisfaction is the response to a single item satisfaction question as shown in table 4-5. Copies of the questionnaires and the actual regression equations used to obtain these results are available from the authors upon request.

Table 4-A
Regression Results for the Effects of Participation
on Various Dependent Variables

Dependent Variable	Not controlling for cross union differences		Controlling for cross union differences	
	Regression coefficient	Standard error	Regression coefficient	Standard error
Interest in Participation				
QWL Issues	0.88	0.55	0.54	0.94
Bread and Butter Issues	1.54**	0.72	1.27	1.20
Strategic Issues	1.12*	0.79	1.16	1.37
Actual Influence				
QWL Issues	1.56**	0.52	0.88	0.90
Bread and Butter Issues	1.70***	0.40	0.54	0.69
Strategic Issues	0.46	0.31	0.28	0.55
Views of Union Performance				
QWL Issues	2.41***	0.64	0.98	1.07
Bread and Butter Issues	2.96***	0.67	0.54	1.12
Strategic Issues	1.41***	0.24	0.20	0.40
Overall Union Performance	0.56*	0.32	0.13	0.23
Views of Job Content	1.80***	0.44	1.62*	1.26

* = significant at 10%.

** = significant at 5%.

*** = significant at 1%.

Chapter 5

Views of Local Union Activists and Officers

Introduction

This chapter presents our findings on the views of local union activists and officers toward worker participation programs. The individuals included in the analysis are elected local officers, executive board members, stewards, members of union committees and, in a few cases, union representatives serving as union "facilitators" of QWL or other participation processes.

The views of these groups are critical for a number of reasons. First, these individuals form the political lifeline of the local union. Opposition from significant numbers of these activists would pose severe political problems for any elected leader who supports the participation process. Second, the responsibilities of these groups span the entire range of union-management relations. Therefore, if any conflicts occur between the participation process and other local union responsibilities (e.g., handling grievances, negotiating local bargaining agreements, etc.), representatives of these groups would be among the first to experience the conflict. Third, in many respects one might predict that union activists are likely to be among the most skeptical critics of

133

worker participation since, like first-line supervisors on the management side, it is their functions that are most directly affected by the move toward broader worker participation and problemsolving. For these reasons, we believe it is critical to understand how union leaders view worker participation processes.

The issues addressed in our analysis include local union leaders' views concerning: (1) the effects of worker participation programs on workplace issues; (2) the effects of the programs on local union officers and election outcomes; (3) the problems which impede the spread or operation of participation programs; and (4) the relationship between worker participation programs and traditional collective bargaining.

The analysis draws from in-depth structured interviews with local union officials from eight industries which recently experimented with one form of participation program or another. In total, approximately 30 individuals were interviewed. In addition, a detailed survey was administered to union officials (executive officers and committeemen) within five auto plants. These plants range from assembly to parts manufacturing facilities and generated approximately 110 responses.

The discussion which follows goes back and forth in reviewing both the quantitative survey responses and the qualitative information gathered in the interviews. In general, the two data sources reveal very similar views. That is, union activists and leaders seem to be telling us the same things in both the interviews and survey.

Effects of Worker Participation Programs
on Workplace Issues

The survey asked union officers in the auto industry to rank the observed effects participation programs have on a wide range of workplace issues on a five point scale ranging from Very Negative Effect, to No Effect, to Very Positive Effect. The responses are reported in table 5-1. The strongest response was registered for Union Officer-Plant Management Relationship, Product/Service Quality, and Productivity where, respectively, 78.3 percent, 74.6 percent and 73.3 percent of the respondents reported the programs had either a Somewhat or Very Positive Effect. For a number of other issues there was a high percentage of union officers who responded there was a Somewhat or Very Positive Effect. The respective percentages were: 72.2 percent for Worker Morale or Job Satisfaction, 73.3 percent for Worker-Supervisor Relations, 64.5 percent for the Grievance Rate, 63.9 percent for Ability to Resolve Grievances, 61.3 percent for Labor Costs, 55.6 percent for Union Member-Shop Committeemen Relations, 55.0 percent for Safety and Health Conditions, and 41.7 percent for the Absenteeism Rate.

There were no workplace issues on which more than 12 percent of the officers thought the participation programs had a Very Negative Effect. The most negative responses appeared in regard to the effects of the programs on Member Satisfaction with the Union and Job Security where, respectively, 32.4 percent and 25.0 percent of the officers thought the program had either Very or Somewhat Negative Effects.

However, union officers frequently did respond that they thought there was No Effect of the programs on some issues. For instance, officers responded that the programs had No Effect on Membership Identification with the Union in 39.8 percent of the responses, and No Effect on Member Satisfaction with the Union in 27.8 percent of the responses. Since these responses raise issues concerning the effect of the programs on the local union, which were questioned in more detail in other sections of the survey, they are discussed more fully later.

Table 5-1
Effects of Participation Programs on Workplace Issues

	Very negative effect	Somewhat negative effect	No effect	Somewhat positive effect	Very positive effect
1. Worker morale or job satisfaction	2.8	12.0	13.0	54.6	17.6
2. Worker-supervisor relations	0.0	14.7	17.4	56.2	17.1
3. Productivity	3.8	5.7	17.1	56.2	17.1
4. Product/service quality	3.8	4.7	17.0	34.0	40.6
5. Labor costs	4.7	5.7	28.3	50.0	11.3
6. Job security	11.1	13.9	36.1	26.9	12.0
7. Union member-shop committeemen relations	1.9	18.5	24.1	42.6	13.0
8. Member satisfaction with the union	6.5	25.9	27.8	31.5	8.3
9. Grievance rate	1.9	4.7	29.0	38.3	26.2
10. Union officer-plant management relationship	1.9	4.7	15.1	49.1	29.2
11. Absenteeism rate	2.8	7.4	48.1	34.3	7.4

12. Safety and health conditions	2.8	2.8	39.4	44.0	11.0
13. Union member-officer relationship	4.7	11.2	34.6	39.3	10.3
14. Membership identification with the union	5.6	17.6	39.8	29.6	7.4
15. Ability to resolve grievances	1.9	8.3	25.9	42.6	21.3

In the interviews, local union officers repeatedly and strongly stated their view that the participation programs had contributed to a significant reduction in the grievance and absentee rates, a statement consistent with the survey responses. A number of union officers stated that recent layoffs which had displaced less senior workers also had contributed to a reduction in grievance and absentee rates. However, they firmly believed that it could be a mistake to attribute the decline in these rates solely to the layoff of less experienced workers. It was their view that the participation programs had significant *independent* impacts on these rate declines.

Union activists were able to cite a number of specific work organization and work process changes which had been identified and adopted through the participation processes. These changes include better lighting, relocation of particular machines, improvements in physical access to machinery, and better coordination between workers. It is their opinion that these changes contributed to both improvements in product quality and costs, and to a resulting enhancement in job security.

Effects on the Local Union

As shown in table 5-2, union activists had a mixed view regarding the effects of worker participation programs on local union affairs. There was some support for the view that the programs had positive effects on the local union. When asked in the survey about the overall effects of the participation programs on the union, 58.0 percent of the officials thought the programs would either probably or definitely strengthen the local union. As one union activist summarized the likely effects of the participation process on his local union,

> Probably strengthen. It's going to give the union guy more say on his job, how it's designed and

Table 5-2
Effects of Participation Programs on Local Union Affairs

	Strongly disagree	Disagree	Neither agree nor disagree	Agree	Strongly agree
1. Interfered with the proper role of the grievance procedure.	23.8	29.5	25.7	18.1	2.9
2. Given workers another channel to get their problems solved.	2.8	5.5	6.4	64.2	21.1
3. Reduced member interest in the union.	17.9	29.2	34.0	13.2	5.7
4. Improved the ability of union representatives to solve problems or complaints workers bring to them.	3.7	14.8	23.1	43.5	14.8
5. Undermined the union's ability to enforce the contract.	28.4	33.9	18.3	13.8	5.5
	Definitely weaken	Probably weaken	No effect	Probably strengthen	Definitely strengthen
6. Improved the union's communications with its members.	2.8	15.0	30.8	36.4	15.0
7. Overall effect of worker participation process on the local union	8.4	12.1	21.5	34.6	23.4

more knowledge of the business. It will hopefully strengthen employment. If job security increases, some credit will go to the union. But the union is not perceived yet as a 50-50 partner with management. The union doesn't have all the training management does.

Another union activist said,

The union's going to change, they won't be so much adversarial. Once they understand the benefits of the process, they will solve a lot of problems easier. If it weakens the union, it weakens today's role, but it can strengthen the future role of being more active between contract times. Now the people have more of a voice, they will learn a lot of skills. For example, people will learn the union system. They're a very strong group of people. I don't think the union leadership really realizes that yet. Only three percent show up at a membership meeting. The union leaders now have to be more exposed, to be part of the people. Otherwise the people say "Hey, you're never there, I never see you."

Union officers also frequently agreed (85.3 percent) with the statement that the participation programs would give workers another channel to get their problems solved, and 62.3 percent disagreed with the statement that the programs would undermine the union's ability to enforce the contract.

There were several individuals who conditioned their judgment of the effects on the local union upon how the union participates in the process. The following statements illustrate this type of response.

If the union realizes the strength of QWL to the people, QWL will probably strengthen the union. It will weaken the union if the union doesn't get more involved with the people within the process.

I guess it depends on the definition of weakness and strength. If we look at the union as encouraging grievances and opposing management, if that's perceived as strength, then I would hope this process would weaken that. I think the role of the union might be strengthened if it evolves into something else, a new role. I'd hope to see lower decision making in the organization so that it will be flatter than it is now, one in which good employees would be given more time and recognition. Now the union is protecting the bad people. If we could better take care of the good, I'll be happy.

There was also a minority viewpoint expressed that the participation programs interfered with proper union activities. Within one auto plant, 6 out of 16 survey respondents agreed with the statement that the participation process "interfered with the proper role of the grievance procedure," while in another plant, 6 out of 24 respondents agreed with that statement. In these two plants, respectively, 19 percent and 25 percent of the survey respondents also agreed with the view that the participation programs "undermined the union's ability to enforce the contract."

As one local union official put it:

Some of the issues being discussed [in the participation program] are in violation of the national agreement and the union's rights as exclusive bargaining agent. The younger people are giving away gains that have been won through much struggle and hardship in the past.

However, in the other plants a lower percentage of surveyed union officials agreed with these statements. Thus, as stated earlier, on average, union leaders disagreed with the view that participation programs either interfered with the proper role of the grievance procedure or undermined the contract.

At the same time, union officers suggested that there was no clear evidence that the participation programs increased member satisfaction or identification with the union. As described earlier, union officers saw little, if any, effect on member satisfaction or member identification with the local union. When asked in the question included in table 5-2 whether the programs reduced member interest in the union, a large percentage of respondents (34.0 percent) neither agreed nor disagreed and few officers witnessed strong effects. However, officers tended to agree (51.4 percent) with the view that the programs improved the union's communication with its members.

Interview data supported this ambiguous assessment of the effect of the worker participation programs on member interest in the local union. Officers repeatedly stated that they saw *no* increase in member participation in union meetings or activities in the aftermath of the creation of participation programs. This is consistent with the worker survey data discussed in chapter 4. Furthermore, union leaders often remarked that any differences in the level of activism in union affairs arose from the fact that union activists are more willing to get involved in participation programs. Hence, the participants always were more involved in union affairs and did not become more involved because of their experiences in worker participation programs.

Some leaders pondered whether additional steps could be taken to inform workers of the local union's role in the participation process. Many officers expressed the view that the programs had little effect on union affairs because members did not perceive or understand the role played by the local union in the programs. To some extent, this may be a consequence of the local union's actions, as union leaders chose not to become clearly identified with participation programs in their early stages because of doubts regarding the ultimate course and worker reaction to the programs. Yet, even in situations where the local union leadership had decided to fully support the participation effort, the leaders often were at a loss to explain why workers did not perceive the union's active role in the programs.

A number of union activists wrestled with the problem of both what to decide regarding the proper separation between collective bargaining and participation programs, and how to maintain any desired level of separation. A variety of approaches had been tried. In one plant explicit lists were kept on what were deemed permissible or "on-line" subjects for consideration in participation processes, and those "off-line" subjects that were deemed to be the domain of collective bargaining. As a participant in this process described it,

> We have an online and an offline sheet. It shows what the teams can work out. If they think an issue is offline, they will get the shop chairman in on a meeting to talk. The people generally listen to supervision when they say "it's offline, it's contractual."

In another plant, union officers monitored the activities of shop floor Quality Circles, a part of the participation program. Whenever a "contractual" issue arose as a topic within a circle, these officials intervened, stopped discussion of the contractual issue, and brought the issue under dispute to the shop committee so it could be resolved through negotiations with management. Then, when the issue was resolved, the settlement terms were brought back to the Quality Circle for implementation.

Another issue we probed was the effects of the participation program on union elections. We found no instances where union officers who strongly supported participation programs had been turned out of office because of that support. Most union officials expressed the view that support for participation programs had been irrelevant to election outcomes. Some officers did state that support for these programs had become an election issue, and that in a few cases this support had, on net, even lost individuals some votes. Yet, consistent with the evidence from the steel industry reported in chapter 3, there were no reports of elections being *decided* on the basis of participation program views.

The operation of worker participation programs typically involves the creation of a set of union and employer representatives who are designated as participation "coordinators" who are responsible for training and advising participation teams in problemsolving activities. This coordinator job creates a new role for union representatives. Since this new job requires the union activists to mediate any tensions between the participation process and traditional bargaining procedures, it is illuminating to look more closely at how these participation coordinators function and what coordinators say about their jobs.

One participation coordinator described his role as follows:

I have a couple of different roles. First, I am a demonstrator of the process, trainer or teacher. That's the fun and easy part. Second, I'm a monitor of the process—living it once you're involved. We interface with so many organizations: engineering, plant manager's staff, materials people. It's a nice job, a learning experience, a continuous high. I enjoy working with people. I held the job of shop chairman before and also enjoyed that job.

Two union coordinators emphasized the intermediary nature of the role they play as facilitator of the participation process.

> We're neither fish nor fowl. We're a buffer zone between the union and management. I try *not* to take a union line or a management line. That's where our strength lies.

> We train one day per week. Initially it was three days per week. We also train the Business Center Steering Committees in groups of three. We train problem solving teams and then we monitor weekly meetings and give followup action to help make sure things are followed through. We also spend a lot of time debating the philosophy of QWL, the change it represents to management—first line, general foremen, and managers. We are constantly in meetings with the plant manager or the personnel director or internal or external consultants.

In contrast to the focus on training, improving communications and problemsolving, and the intermediary nature of the coordinators' role, the shop chairmen describe their jobs as more focused on the enforcement and protection of worker rights under the collective bargaining agreement. Still, however, there are common problemsolving functions that cut across these two positions.

Consider, for example, the following description of his job provided by one shop chairman.

> A lot of times I act as a peacemaker, a lot of times it is *not* tied into grievances. Some issues are contractual and you have to get the message through. Lots of times people don't like contractual wording. You have to make a decision of right versus wrong. I also have a lot of personal relationships with union members. They need somebody to

talk to regarding personal problems. I handled disputes between management and union personnel on problems. I solve a lot of problems before they are grievances.

We asked participation coordinators to compare their job to that of union committeemen. Below are some statements by coordinators which illustrate their perceptions of the similarities and differences in these two union positions.

They are similar in that sometimes I feel like an arbitrator when people have a bitch about something. They are different—we have more positives than negatives. The shop chairman's called when something goes wrong. We are helping people to develop—that's a big role—and the shop chairman doesn't.

The shop chairmen only deal with the "five percenters." The shop chairman is there to preserve jobs. You don't have the time to associate with the other 95%. As a trainer I'm now associated with all the kinds of people that are generally concerned about their job and their organization. They have the same goals and objectives that I have in my job.

Problems Impeding the Expansion of Participation Programs

Union officials were asked in the survey to weigh the importance of various factors as problems that limited the expansion of participation programs. Their responses are reported in table 5-3. The factors that were ranked as the biggest problems were layoffs, management efforts to change work rules or practices, and supervisor resentment or resistance. Respectively, 53.2 percent, 44.4 percent and 42.8 percent of the respondents thought these problems had

Table 5-3

Problems that Limit the Expansion of the Participation Process

	Not at all	Somewhat	Quite a bit	A very great deal
Worker disenchantment	3.8	61.9	23.8	10.5
Supervisor resentment or resistance	10.5	46.7	29.5	13.3
Loss of union support	54.7	35.8	7.5	1.9
Loss of plant management support	43.0	37.4	11.2	8.4
Conflict between workers and supervisors	12.4	57.1	21.9	8.6
Management efforts to change work rules or practices	7.4	48.1	32.4	12.0
Layoffs or other employment cutbacks	19.6	27.1	28.0	25.2
Disruptions of groups caused by worker transfers to different jobs	21.3	40.7	25.9	12.0

limited the expansion of the program either quite a bit or a very great deal.

The interviews were consistent with these survey responses. Union officials repeatedly stated that a chief problem in the participation process was resistance encountered in the ranks of middle management. As one union official put it,

> Front-line managers don't endorse it [worker participation]. The Vice President and President think it's great, but the word has not filtered down to foremen that it is going to be a management policy.

A number of union officials asserted that the continuing economic decline in their industry had led to member frustration and disenchantment with the participation process. These officials suggested that unless participants saw some clear gains from participation, activity levels eventually declined. Here, the problem was that deterioration of the larger economic environment overwhelmed many of the immediate short-run improvements of the participation process. Thus, although these improvements were real and valued, it was difficult to sustain the energy needed to support participatory programs in the face of continued large scale layoffs.

External events also affected workers' willingness to engage in cooperative efforts with management. In one plant, a union officer suggested that worker interest in participation programs waned considerably when management began to move business out of the plant and into a nonunion southern facility. As noted in chapter 3, some workers in steel plants were hesitant to commit themselves to a participation process because of their suspicion that management would utilize any cost savings generated by these programs to invest more heavily in businesses other than the steel industry.

Overall Assessment and Thoughts
Regarding the Future

In general, union activists and officials had a very positive attitude toward worker participation programs. Union officials frequently stated that they were in favor of workers participating more directly in production decisionmaking and were in favor of workers gaining wider input into the determination of their working conditions. When asked whether they advised workers to actively participate in the program, 81.7 percent indicated that they encourage workers to participate (see table 5-4). When asked what the union's role in the participation process should be, 84.3 percent of the union officials said the union should support and actively participate in running the program with management.

Another issue relates to the future course of their worker participation programs. When asked about what kind of participation process would likely be around in five years, 65.1 percent of the surveyed local union officials in the auto industry held the view that the participation process will have grown and expanded (table 5-4). To probe this issue, we asked in the interviews how either a new economic boom or further decline in economic conditions would affect the course of the participation program. Some officials expressed the view that a strong economic recovery would probably lead management to be less concerned with the participation programs and their associated emphasis on improved product quality, and rather would lead to the return of an emphasis on "getting it out the door." Yet, if this were to occur, these union leaders generally believed workers would resent any management efforts to roll back worker participation and, in fact, "would just not let it happen." This supported their claim that they and the workforce truly valued the additional input received via the participation programs, and hence would not willingly let such programs dissipate.

Table 5-4
Overall Views of the Participation Programs

Question: What do you think the union's role ought to be in the participation process?

3.7	The union should oppose the program.
12.0	The union should remain neutral but not actively participate in the process.
84.3	The union should support and actively participate in running the program with management.

Question: If we were to come back five years from now, what kind of participation process do you think we would find here?

13.8	The participation process will have ended by then.
21.1	The participation process will look about the same as it is today.
65.1	The participation process will have grown and expanded.

Question: If workers ask you about whether they should participate in the participation program, what do you generally advise?

81.7	I encourage them to participate.
17.4	I don't take a position one way or the other.
.9	I discourage them from participating.

Union officials' views regarding the likely course of events if the participation process actually took hold and expanded differed according to their views regarding the role of these participation programs. Some officials viewed the participation process as a useful but limited complement to the collective bargaining process. In their eyes, the proper role of participation programs is to provide a supplementary channel through which workers could provide suggestions regarding working conditions on those issues where there were clear gains to be had by both sides. In line with this role, these union leaders thought that even if participation programs flourished, they always would have a limited function. In this case, these programs would not preclude the operation of the collective bargaining process, and the local union's place in the bargaining process would continue in much the same fashion as before introduction of the worker participation program.

Some other union officials envisioned the possible expansion of the participation process to the point that workers would carry out many of the responsibilities now held by supervisors and middle management. In this scenario, the participation process would come to play a much more integral role in the determination of work conditions and thereby take over some, and possibly many, of the functions now performed by collective bargaining. These local officials speculated that the local union's role might then shift toward representation of either wider community interests at the workplace or towards greater satisfaction of the career goals or nonwork-related interests of their membership.

Chapter 6

Views from the Top of the Labor Movement*

The purpose of this chapter is to review the contemporary thinking of key national labor movement leaders on worker participation issues. We will draw on data from interviews, speeches, other public documents and selected internal union documents to understand how the top of the labor movement views worker participation.

While the worker participation processes studied in this book are inherently local activities, leaders of national unions and of higher level union federations such as the AFL-CIO influence participation processes in at least two important ways. First, through their public statements national labor leaders mold the public's perceptions of the attitude of the labor movement toward worker participation and quality of working life improvement efforts. While the public's perceptions are perhaps not critical in any direct way, two specific groups of interest to the labor movement may listen with greater attentiveness, namely, unorganized workers whom unions would like to recruit and high level executives who shape their firm's strategies toward unions and worker participation programs. Thus, the public statements

---

*We wish to thank Alan Birbaum for collecting much of the background data for this chapter while he was a student intern at the Industrial Union Department of the AFL-CIO in 1982.

of labor leaders are important in shaping the overall image of the labor movement in the minds of at least these two key groups.

Second, top union leaders are responsible for shaping the overall strategy of their organizations toward worker participation and designing an organizational structure capable of implementing that strategy down through the union to its grass roots level. The structure put into place will in turn serve as the channel of information from local to top union leaders. For these reasons, therefore, it is important to understand how national level labor leaders are responding to the question of whether worker participation processes are, indeed, a threat or an opportunity for their organizations.

The AFL-CIO

The AFL-CIO does not have any official policy on QWL or any other form of worker participation program. This is consistent with its historical role in the structure of the American labor movement since the AFL-CIO does not directly negotiate nor administer collective bargaining agreements. Instead, its role is to provide political leadership to the labor movement, to share information, to coordinate the efforts of the various national unions, and to provide staff assistance and advice to national and regional affiliates. Consistent with their leadership role, however, from time to time the president and secretary-treasurer of the AFL-CIO have outlined their personal views on the matter of worker participation. Most recently, the clearest and most detailed statement was provided by Mr. Thomas Donahue, secretary-treasurer of the AFL-CIO. The central points contained in his January 1982 speech to a QWL conference are summarized below.[1]

Donahue indicated to the group that, as noted above, the Federation has no policy on quality of worklife programs and believes it is more appropriate to leave it to each national union to chart its own course after considering the types of employers it deals with.

> For strong unions, able to insist on an equal and active voice in how the program works, or able, if necessary, to veto actions that aim at subverting its bargaining position, [QWL] isn't an insuperable problem. That accounts for the general acceptance of quality of worklife programs by such dominant and secure unions as the Auto Workers, Steel Workers, and Communications Workers. Even they have sometimes had to take strong action to prevent their employers from using the programs as conduits for company propaganda in bargaining situations.

A second key point stressed by Donahue was that while collective bargaining will always remain an adversarial process, i.e., the basic conflict of interests between workers and employers will not go away because of worker participation or cannot be wished away by QWL advocates, the conflict should be limited to the negotiation of the labor agreement. During the period of the contract there should be room for cooperation.

> I do believe that the adversarial role, appropriate to the conflict of collective bargaining, ought to be limited to the period of negotiation—and during the lifetime of a contract so arrived at, it ought to be replaced by a period of cooperation, aimed at maximizing the potential success of the joint enterprise, i.e., the company's business or production.

Above all, Donahue stressed that any QWL or other worker participation process should be viewed as a supplement to, not a replacement for, the collective bargaining process—"the collective bargaining process is the cornerstone to honest labor-management cooperation." He also warned against elevating QWL efforts to the status of a "movement" or a "philosophical belief." Instead, he prefers to treat them for what they are—experiments designed to improve productivity and quality and the satisfaction of workers with their jobs.

In summary, Donahue's approach is one of cautious skepticism. He is skeptical because he recognizes that American employers have embraced worker participation most recently during times of economic adversity as part of their efforts to regain a stronger competitive position. Other employers are using employee involvement strategies to keep unions out of their organizations. These two facts are consistent with employer behavior at earlier points in American labor history—labor and management have banded together to cooperate during periods of economic or military crisis only to return to more open periods of conflict when the crisis eased. Thus, collective bargaining is viewed as a more flexible and appropriate instrument for dealing with American employers; it allows unions to exert an independent voice for employee interests in whatever fashion works most effectively given the existing environment.

Finally, Donahue noted the biggest obstacle to the development of a more lasting form of labor-management cooperation in the U.S.:

> I might note parenthetically that the ability of the trade union movement as a whole to sense a partnership would be vastly enlarged by the elimination by management of the "Union-Free Environment" mentality which nowadays so apparently affects thousands of employers, large and small, and leaves the trade union movement embattled and badly disposed to cooperate on the macro-economic and political issues which could benefit from such an approach.

> We [the labor movement] have long demonstrated our willingness to join with management in developing more prosperous communities and in revitalizing our industries, and we'll continue to do so. What we expect in return is a little less short-term manipulation and more fidelity in the relationship over the long haul.

As we review the diversity of views of other national union leaders, we will see that despite differences of opinion on other matters, all are in essential accord with this basic point.

Representative Views of National Unions

We will now turn to a survey of the views and perspectives on worker participation issues found across different national unions. These views are generally captured by four different approaches which are discussed below. As illustrated in figure 6-1, the continuum of views across national unions ranges from general opposition to general endorsement of worker participation strategies. In between these two extremes are two decentralized policies. One is a general policy of leaving the decision of how to respond to worker participation programs entirely to the local unions. The other is a modified decentralized policy of leaving it up to the locals, but providing national level staff and/or elected leaders who both promote the development of worker participation processes and provide expert assistance to locals interested in implementing specific processes. For each of these types we will summarize some of the approaches of specific unions.

General Opposition: The Case of the IAM

The clearest case of a union that is generally opposed to worker participation processes as they are currently carried out is the International Association of Machinists and

Figure 6-1
Representative Views of National Unions
on Worker Participation

General Opposition

* outspoken critics
* resist initial involvement
* end any ongoing programs
* collective bargaining is sufficient
* joint committees may be acceptable

Decentralized Neutrality

* leave decision entirely to local unions
* no statement of general opposition or support
* no international staff support or leadership to interested locals
* provide locals with summaries of related research
* provide locals with checklist of suggested questions to answer prior to start-up of project

Decentralized Policy with National Union Support

* leave decision to local unions
* promote development and provide assistance in implementation through international level staff and leaders
* encourage local union experimentation
* no public endorsement by International president
* articulate national promoters
* letters of understanding between parties in bargaining agreements

General Endorsement

* support from the International president
* promote development and provide assistance in implementation through international level staff and leaders
* encourage local union experimentation

Increasing Support for Worker Participation

Aerospace Workers (IAM). The president of the IAM, William Winpisinger, was an early outspoken critic of QWL programs when they were first introduced into U.S. industry in the early 1970s and continues to be their harshest contemporary critic.[2] IAM policy toward QWL and QC programs is outlined in a 1982 letter from Winpisinger to IAM local lodges.[3] The letter suggests the following guidelines for local leaders who need to decide how to respond to QWL types of programs in their plants.

> *First,* notify the management that under IAM policy every aspect of the employer-employee relationship is subject to negotiation through collective bargaining.

> *Second,* warn members to watch for dilution of contract clauses governing job description, training, wage structure, promotion, benefits, grievance procedures or other factors normally decided through collective bargaining.

> *Third,* set up a watchdog committee within the lodge to monitor quality of worklife committees.

> *Fourth,* keep Grand Lodge informed of your experiences with quality of worklife programs.

A discussion with George Poulin, general vice-president of the IAM, further clarified the international's policy toward worker participation.[4] The union's first preference would be for its members and local leaders not to get involved in these programs in the first place and to bring an end to them where they have started. The IAM believes that it has not seen any issues raised by QWL programs which cannot be effectively dealt with through collective bargaining.

If the participation effort continues to exist in an IAM facility, its representatives are advised to proceed as follows:

1. Guarantees should be obtained that the process will not in any way circumvent the negotiations process or the collective bargaining agreement.

2. Union stewards should participate and be involved in all discussions of the QWL groups and play a watchdog role to insure the agreement or the rights of any workers are not violated.

3. No workers should be laid off as a result of recommendations or decisions of the participation process.

4. Management should agree to negotiate all aspects of the issues discussed in the participation process. That is, if the union agrees to open itself up to discussions that may introduce changes in practices within the bargaining unit, then management should also be willing to discuss aspects of issues that traditionally have been treated as managerial prerogatives.

This fourth condition is a key to understanding the views of the IAM. In contrast to its stated opposition to QWL programs, this union has been a leader in calling for full joint discussions of the use of new technology. It has proclaimed a "Workers' Technology Bill of Rights" for the introduction of new technology, reproduced in figure 6-2.[5] One of the central points contained in this statement on technology is that employers and union representatives should consult on all aspects of the decision to introduce new technology from the earliest stage of the employer's decisionmaking process. Thus, the IAM is not opposed to union-employer joint programs per se. Instead, it supports joint discussions which it believes allow the union to participate as a full joint partner in all aspects of the issues involved.

Poulin summarized another important reason for the IAM's general opposition to cooperative programs with employers:

Basically, the whole issue comes down to one word: recognition. Employers can have it either way but they can't walk down both sides of the aisle. If they want cooperation, they have to be willing to fully accept unions. On the other hand, if they want to engage in a ten to fifteen year fight to see who comes out on top, they can have that too. But we cannot help them to destroy us slowly by cooperating in specific plants while they screw us out of others. The day that the employers in this country truly accept the right of unions to exist we will see more changes than anyone could ever believe.

Our problem is that there is always a hidden agenda [in the minds of employers]. Employers have trained us well to know this. They were our teachers and we have learned this lesson again and again over the years in the school of hard knocks.

The IAM strategy toward QWL and related workplace cooperative efforts is part of the union's larger industrial strategy for revitalizing American industry and reforming national economic policy. For example, Winpisinger's comments on the viability of business-labor-government cooperative efforts at the national level of the economy are fully consistent with the IAM policy toward joint cooperative efforts with specific employers at the workplace:

Since [European style] social-contract systems work elsewhere and our employers profitably live with them in other countries where they invest, we can demand no less here in America. This is where the discussion of cooperation must begin. In plainer words, the business community and the Government must call off their antiunion and antisocial dogs. It is unreasonable to expect cooperation on the part of workers in the workplace, only to find a management, in complicity with Government, stabbing them in the back and cutting the safety net out from under them in the policy outside the plant gate or office. Cooperation requires good faith on the part of all parties. It is a two-way street.[6]

Figure 6-2
International Association of Machinists Statement
on Workers' Technology Bill of Rights

Amend National Labor Relations Act, Railway Labor Act, and other appropriate acts to declare national policy through a new Technology Bill of Rights:

   I. New Technology shall be used in a way that does not decrease jobs, but creates or maintains jobs and promotes community-wide and national full employment.

  II. Unit cost savings and labor productivity gains resulting from the use of New Technology shall be shared with production workers at the local level and shall not be permitted to accrue solely for the gain of capital, management and shareholders.

Increased leisure time resulting from New Technology shall result in no loss of real income or decline in living standards.

III. Since the greater part of local, state and national tax revenues come from taxes on labor, communities and the nation have the right to require employers to pay a Robot Tax, as a replacement tax, on all machinery, equipment, and production systems that displace workers and cause unemployment.

IV. New Technology shall improve the conditions of work and shall enhance and expand the opportunities for knowledge, skills and compensation of workers. Displaced workers shall not be penalized with loss of income and shall be entitled to training and retraining.

  V. New Technology shall be used to develop the U.S. industrial base, consistent with the Full Employment goal, before it is licensed or exported abroad.

VI. New Technology shall be evaluated in terms of workers' safety and health and shall not be destructive of the workplace environment, nor shall it be used at the expense of the community's natural environment.

VII. Workers, through their trade unions and bargaining units, shall have an absolute right to participate in all phases of management deliberations and decisions that lead or could lead to the introduction of New Technology or the changing of the workplace system design, work processes and procedures for doing work, including the shutdown or transfer or work, capital, plant and equipment.

VIII. Workers shall have the right to monitor control room centers and control stations and the New Technology shall not be used to monitor, measure or otherwise control the work practices and work standards of individual workers, at the point of work.

IX. Storage of an individual worker's personal data and information file by the employer shall be tightly controlled and the collection and/or release and dissemination of information with respect to race, religious or political activities and beliefs, records of physical and mental health disorders and treatments, records of arrests and felony charges or convictions, information concerning sexual preferences and conduct, information concerning internal and private family matters, and information regarding an individual's financial condition or credit worthiness shall not be permitted, except in rare circumstances related to health, and then only after consultation with a family or union-appointed physician, psychiatrist or member of the clergy.

The right of the individual worker to inspect his or her own personal data file shall at all times be absolute and open to him or her.

X. When the New Technology is employed in the production of military goods and services, workers, through their trade union and bargaining agent, have a right to bargain with management over the establishment of Alternative Production Committees, which shall design ways to adopt that technology to socially-useful production and products in the civilian sector of the economy.

SOURCE: *Let's Rebuild America,* International Association of Machinists, 1983, Appendix B.

Decentralized Neutrality

Perhaps the dominant national union strategy toward worker participation can be described as decentralized neutrality. That is, while national leaders speak out from time to time for or against QWL or other worker participation efforts, each local of the national union is left to decide generally on its own, in accordance with its own needs and preferences, how to respond to employer initiatives in this area. Under this strategy no high ranking national union leaders or staff specialists are identified as public supporters of worker participation and no staff specialists are assigned specific responsibility for encouraging locals to get involved in joint efforts or assisting them when the issue comes up.

Some of the unions that follow this genuinely neutral and decentralized strategy have provided locals with summaries of research on participation. The IUE, for example, has done this. The guidelines that its local unions are encouraged to follow are reproduced in figure 6-3 for local unions.

Other unions such as the Allied Industrial Workers (AIW) provide locals with a checklist of suggested questions to ask itself and the employer before embarking on a joint program (see figure 6-4).

Many of the unions that follow this strategy of decentralized neutrality, such as the IUE, the AIW, and the UFCW, deal with a large and very diverse range of employers, none of which employ a majority of the national union's members. For this reason, it is difficult for national union leaders to announce one single policy that fits each situation. What sets these unions apart from the IAM on the one hand, and the unions that will be classified in the two remaining categories on the other, is that they have neither stated a general opposition to workplace level participation, nor provided international staff support or leadership to locals that show an interest in pursuing a joint program.

Figure 6-3
IUE Guidelines for Local Union Participation
in Quality Circles

1. Go slowly. Make sure the Quality Circle idea is not just a gimmick of management to improve its own position. Make sure, too, that union membership knows what Quality Circles are designed to accomplish.

2. Be sure the union is an equal partner in the Quality Circle program. In this way, the union can insure that its interests and the interests of its members are protected and respected.

3. Be sure that any management initiation of Quality Circles can deliver *top* management support—and that means demanding meetings with top management. Union leadership does not want to go out on a limb with its membership and endorse something that is later discontinued.

4. Get assurance that the Circle will not be involved with conditions of employment and work which is provided for in the terms of the collective bargaining agreement. One way of insuring this is to make certain that Quality Circle facilitators and leaders are adequately and properly trained.

5. To protect its membership, unions must get some guarantee that the implementation of Quality Circles does not eliminate jobs. These guarantees should be put in writing.

6. Unions must be assured that the adoption of Quality Circles does not turn into a *speed-up*.

7. Unions must insist that management maintains a *balance between the two aims of the program:* management benefits and worker benefits.

8. Unions must insist that savings resulting from the Circles must be *shared with employees.* Unions need to ask:
   * Are savings being used to improve the company's operation?
   * Are savings going to be returned to the workers in improved benefits?

Once the Quality Circle is set in motion, the union must:

   * Insist workers who take time off for Quality Circles be paid for that time.

   * Keep workers fully informed on all activities beginning with the first meeting with management.

   * Insist on union representation at every Circle.

* Provide initially for access to company data.

* Make certain there is an organized evaluation system to see if the program is serving its agreed-upon purpose.

* Make sure there is a clear understanding of *operational* procedures on both sides.

* Communication is the most important ingredient.

  * One suggestion has been that the union start with a survey of the membership to determine their needs and interests.

  * Another is to get an agreement to *periods of discussion* on the proposed program.

  * A third is to insist that bulletin boards be placed throughout the plant to post exclusively what is developing (or taking place) within Quality Circles.

And, finally, local unions should keep their Internationals informed of the establishment of Quality Circles so that the Union can keep track of, as well as develop an analysis of, the impact of these on its members.

SOURCE: "Quality of Working Life Outline," International Union of Electrical, Radio and Machine Workers, internal document, no date.

Figure 6-4
Allied Industrial Workers Checklist on Quality Circles

Some Important Questions to Ask
Regarding the Implementation and Operation
of Quality Control Circles at Your Plant

I. Prior History

A. Prior to the introduction of a Quality Control Circle program at your location, was your relationship with the Company cooperative?

B. Did the Company propose language for economic concessions during the last round of negotiations?

C. Did the Company try to settle most grievances at the lower steps of the grievance procedure or force most to the final step?

D. Prior to initiating QCCs did the Company participate on any joint committees with the Union, for example, a joint health and safety committee?

II. Program Introduction

A. Was the QCC program discussed with local Union officers prior to being announced to the general membership?

B. How much information did the Company give the Union prior to introducing the program?

C. Was the Local Union involved in discussions to determine the priority problems which would be addressed by the QCCs?

D. Was the Union involved in the initial QCC orientation program?

E. Was the Union involved in discussing the procedures that would be adopted in order to implement the program?

III. Implementation and Operation

A. Is the Union officially represented on the QCC Steering Committee?

B. Are there an equal number of labor and management representatives on the Steering Committee?

C. Is the Union involved as an equal partner in each Circle orientation program?

IV. Program Evaluation

A. Prior to the introduction of QCC did the Company provide the Union with a statement, with supporting data, as to the problems they were trying to solve?

B. Has there been any discussion between the Company and the Union as to how the program will be evaluated? That is, how will success or failure be measured?

C. Is the Union involved in the evaluation procedure and receiving all material related to the evaluation?

D. Does the Union receive minutes of all Circle and Steering Committee meetings and related correspondence?

V. Impact on Collective Bargaining

A. Is there a written agreement between the Company and the Local Union which specifies that the QCC program will not deal with subjects covered by the Collective Bargaining agreement?

B. Has there been any noticeable change in management's behavior in handling grievances?

C. Has there been a decline in grievance activity since the introduction of the Quality Circle program?

D. Will the introduction of this Quality Circle program pose any problems for your next round of negotiations?

E. Is there the potential that the introduction of a Quality Control Circle program will interfere with the administration of the Collective Bargaining agreement?

VI. Union Management Cooperation

A. During the implementation of the QCC program did the local propose any changes in the workplace which would solve some of its problems?

B. What are some of the local issues which you feel could be proposed to management as an indicator of management's "cooperative spirit?"

SOURCE: Research Department, Allied Industrial Workers, 1983.

Decentralized Policy with National Union Support

A third group of unions, most notably the UAW and the USW, encourage local union experimentation with worker participation and have one or more high level international union leaders and/or staff representatives who serve as active promoters and supporters of such efforts. However, public endorsement of participation stops short of the office of the international president of these unions. To understand the nature of the support provided by these unions, we will review in some detail the history of the roles of worker participation in the UAW and the USW.

The UAW. The earliest articulate spokesman for QWL programs within the labor movement was Irving Bluestone, who served, until his retirement in 1979, as the UAW vice-president for the General Motors Department. Bluestone was the driving force behind the negotiation of the first QWL clause to be included in a national level bargaining agreement. Largely at his insistence, the following letter of understanding was appended to the 1973 agreement between the UAW and General Motors:

> In discussions prior to the opening of the current negotiations for a new collective bargaining agreement, General Motors Corporation and the UAW gave recognition to the desirability of mutual effort to improve the quality of work life for the employees. In consultation with Union representatives, certain projects have been undertaken by management in the field of organizational development, involving the participation of represented employees. These and other projects and experiments which may be undertaken in the future are designed to improve the quality of work life, thereby advantaging the worker by making work a

more satisfying experience, advantaging the Corporation by leading to a reduction in employee absenteeism and turnover, and advantaging the consumer through improvement in the quality of the products manufactured.

As a result of these earlier discussions and further discussions during the course of the current negotiations for a new collective bargaining agreement, the parties have decided that a Committee to Improve the Quality of Work Life composed of representatives of the International Union and General Motors will be established at the national level.

This Committee will meet periodically and have responsibility for:

1. Reviewing and evaluating programs of the Corporation which involve improving the work environment of employees represented by the UAW.

2. Developing experiments and projects in that area.

3. Maintaining records of its meetings, deliberations and all experiments and evaluations it conducts.

4. Making reports to the Corporation and the Union on the results of its activities.

5. Arranging for any outside counselling which it feels is necessary or desirable with the expenses thereof to be shared equally by the Corporation and the Union.

The Corporation agrees to request and encourage its plant managements to cooperate in the conduct of such experiments and projects, and recognizes that cooperation by its plant floor supervision is essential to success of this program.

The Union agrees to request and encourage its members and their local union representatives to cooperate in such experiments and projects, and recognizes that the benefits which can flow to employees as a result of successful experimentation is dependent on the cooperation and participation of those employees and the local union representatives.[7]

Since the signing of this agreement in 1973, the UAW and General Motors have participated in an ongoing QWL program and have carried out the intent of this letter by encouraging the development of QWL programs throughout GM plants. Bluestone served as the key union proponent for QWL and advisor to the local unions as they embarked on their own experiments. Although the same basic letter of agreement and national committee structure were included in the Ford and Chrysler agreements with the UAW, Chrysler has yet to actively embark on a vigorous joint participation effort with the UAW. Ford and the UAW only began implementing this language since 1979, when Donald Ephlin became UAW vice-president for the Ford Department (see chapter 3). Thus, the UAW is an example of a major national union that has encouraged the spread of worker participation projects from the top levels of the union.

Still, however, none of the three UAW presidents who held office from 1973 to the present time (Leonard Woodcock, Douglas Fraser, and Owen Bieber) have taken the lead as the spokesman for the desirability of participating in joint workplace participation programs. Instead, they have left it to the international vice-presidents, such as Bluestone and Ephlin, to serve as the union's publicly recognized proponents of this concept. A recent statement of Bluestone's to a GM-UAW plant QWL team perhaps best captures his personal views and the views of the UAW as expressed over the years by these two vice-presidents.

In my thirty-eight years with the UAW, I participated in countless hard core bargaining sessions with General Motors Corporation at both the national level and the local plant level. The collective bargaining relationship in the U.S. is characterized by an adversarial climate, strong debate over highly controversial issues, and occasional crises. In the years ahead the adversarial aspects of labor-management relationships will no doubt continue to play a significant role in advancing the standard of living of workers and their families in improving the working conditions.

It is equally true, however, that a vast array of subjects related to managing the work place and managing the enterprise are, indeed, not adversarial in nature, but are subject to joint problem-solving efforts as matters of common and mutual concern. As to these issues the negotiating parties have a stake in undertaking, jointly, initiatives which are designed to achieve mutually desirable objectives.

Solving problems at the work place should not lie solely in the domain of managerial prerogatives. In fact, in its practical application, problem solving must be rooted in a process which affords workers the opportunity for meaningful participation in the decision-making process. In this sense, "improving the quality of work life" represents a further step toward fulfillment of a persistent, historic objective of unionism: to bring, to the extent feasible, democratic values and procedures into the work place.[8]

In this same speech, Bluestone went on to state, as other union leaders have who are more skeptical of QWL, that there will always be a need for collective bargaining. He went farther, however, than most other labor leaders are yet willing to go, by endorsing the notion that under appropriate circumstances, QWL processes should be allowed to modify terms of the collective bargaining process, and indeed serve as the avenue by which changes in the basic terms of the employment contract are arrived at.

> Unions have and will always have the legal and moral responsibility to protect fairly and aggressively the rights of their members. There will be a continuing need to utilize a grievance procedure and engage in collective bargaining negotiation. The representation collective bargaining role of the union cannot be jeopardized.

> This is not to say that collective bargaining agreements cannot be altered to meet mutually desirable objectives of the QWL process, subject of course to the bargaining process and membership ratification. At Livonia, (a Cadillac engine plant) for example, the traditional wage and classification structure was altered to accommodate the pay-for-knowledge wage system. I expect the natural progression will lead to gain-sharing programs, in which the workers receive financial or other benefits as their fair share in the improved performance of the enterprise.

This is more than a subtle difference from the statements of other labor leaders. It recognizes that QWL efforts can evolve into more than a supplement to collective bargaining and not always remain totally subservient to the terms of the bargaining agreement. In this view, worker participation processes can serve over time as vehicles for proposing major modifications in the bargaining agreement. The only constraint is that any actual changes in the agreement must be negotiated and approved, as would any other modification.

The Bluestone/Ephlin UAW view of the role of worker participation has expanded in another important way. No longer is QWL, or Employee Involvement (EI) as it is called at Ford, viewed as an isolated experiment limited only to the workplace level of the bargaining relationship. Instead, involvement of workers and their employers at the local level is viewed as an integral piece of the larger company and union effort to return the American automobile industry to a position of competitiveness, profitability, and growth. At Ford, for example, the EI process is only the most micro part of an integrated set of structures and practices for information sharing and consultation at the plant- and company-wide levels of the bargaining relationship. It was the positive experiences with the workplace level EI processes at Ford between 1979 and 1982 that set the stage for the 1982 Ford-UAW agreement that provided for these higher levels of consultation as well as expanded joint efforts at retraining and efforts to negotiate pilot employment guarantee programs in selected plants.

The USW. Like the UAW, the USW international office has been actively promoting the diffusion of worker participation processes (called Labor-Management Participation Teams or LMPTs) since the signing of the 1980 bargaining agreement with major employers in the steel industry (see chapter 3). Responsibility for encouraging and monitoring the development of LMPTs is assigned at the national level of the USW to Mr. Sam Camens, special assistant to the president. Like Bluestone, Camens sees workplace participation teams as a logical step toward the development of full-fledged industrial democracy.[9]

He also sees the LMPT experiments as the first step in an evolving process that will eventually modify the basic nature of the employment relationship and the role of management, unions, and workers.

> I tell companies don't start this process if you think you can stop it. By that I mean the process takes on a life and a direction of its own and will increase the interest of workers in participation as they get experience with it. It also helps to cut out a lot of the red tape and standardization and bureaucratization within management.

> It has to be a cultural change. I don't think enough people understand what labor-management participation is all about. It is not simply labor-management cooperation or collaboration. If that's what people think it is it won't amount to anything. We might get to more collaboration and cooperation through participation but the basic thing that participation must do is to break down the barriers between workers and supervisors and the rest of management. Unless this is treated as a cultural change it will not work. It also has to be a part of a trade union's strategy—part of the drive for union and worker democracy. It has to be part of our strategy to stem the losses of young members.[10]

Thus, Camens—like Bluestone and Ephlin at the UAW, and as we will see shortly, Glen Watts at the CWA—believes worker participation must become part of the overall strategy of the labor movement for reforming the employment relationship and for organizing new union members. Yet, these beliefs still constitute a minority view within both the UAW and the USW. They have not been publicly embraced by the presidents of either the USW or the UAW, nor have they been officially built into the general policy statements of either union. The USW, for example, formally endorsed the use of LMPTs for "distressed" industries and firms (i.e., those in serious economic trouble and in need of cooperative efforts from the union and the workers to regain competitive health), but it chose to leave any mention of worker participation out of its statement of bargaining priorities for firms and industries not currently in financial trouble. Lynn Williams, secretary/treasurer of the USW stated the current views of leaders within this union as follows:

> . . . . the majority of the people in the union still see [worker participation] as a strategy for helping those companies in crisis and do not see it as a natural part of an overall strategy for healthy situations. This point of view probably captures the position of most of our top leaders. Our leadership in general is very supportive of the concept of labor-management participation teams *because* of the severe crisis.
>
> There is another group within the union that is very supportive of the concept of labor-management participation in general. This group has a long history within the Steelworkers. One can go back to the days of Phillip Murray (the first president of the Steelworkers) and find a statement of his that endorsed worker participation as his program for economic recovery. The Scanlon Plan came out of the Steelworkers. David MacDonald was an active supporter of human relations and labor-management cooperation. I.W. Abel endorsed and supported the concept of productivity and job security committees and joint efforts at the plant level.
>
> Finally, there is a third group that is extremely committed to the concept of worker participation as a means of extending industrial democracy to the

American workplace. Sam Camens best reflects this point of view within our union.

My own view is that there will always be two elements to the role of unions. One is to help increase the size of the pie and the other is to use collective bargaining to divide up the pie. Traditionally, the union has approached this first task mostly at the very macro levels of the economy through its political lobbying and support for national policy that will promote the growth of the American steel industry. The tri-partite steel committee that was active during the Carter Administration is an example of this. I see the labor-management participation teams at the plant level as the enterprise counterpart efforts to increase the size of the pie. Over the long run I think these two functions will fit together comfortably in the union's strategy.[11]

In summary, both the USW and the UAW have articulate national promoters of worker participation. In both cases, however, the spokesmen are one step removed from the office of the international union president. Both unions also have assigned national level staff people to assist locals in developing participation programs and have put considerable resources of the national union into training its staff and supporting local union participation activities.

Support from the President: The CWA

At this point in time, only one president of a major international union has publicly gone on record as supporting the introduction of worker participation efforts as an integral part of the union's long-run strategy. Glen Watts, president of the CWA, summarized his views and the posture of the CWA in a recent speech to a national conference on labor-management cooperation.

. . . . aspects of QWL are seen by many in the labor movement as a threat. But others—and I include myself among them—see it as offering a great opportunity to extend the reach of collective bargaining.

Labor is concerned with the development of democracy in industry. The collective bargaining process will always be the foundation of industrial democracy; but QWL gives us the tools to build higher than we ever have before.

. . . . collective bargaining has not been weakened. We work on the traditional issues of wages and basic working conditions just as we always have.

But through QWL, we are extending our influence into the murky territory of "management prerogatives," help-to-shape management practices and policies while they are being formed rather than after the fact.

In the long run, I believe this cannot help but strengthen the union. That is why we have committed significant resources and effort to QWL.[12]

Like his more skeptical colleagues within the labor movement, Watts recognizes that many employers and some consultants use QWL as strategies for avoiding or undermining unions. He likewise condemns the use of participation strategies for these purposes. However, he favors a different response than some to this tactical use of QWL:

Now I want to come back for a moment to the other kind of QWL—the gimmicky type—the kind that aims at narrow productivity goals or undercuts unions. What should Labor's stand be toward these?

I don't think it is sufficient to stand on the sidelines and attack management's motives. That strategy puts unions on the defensive and makes management appear more concerned about workers than we are.

. . . . our experience, along with that of the UAW and the Steelworkers, has provided us a new strategy.

We have a way of telling good programs from bad programs. We can offer our own Labor model of a good QWL process as a challenge to management. We know that a good worker participation process involves some basic elements, which I will repeat:

1. Protection of worker rights, especially the rights to job security and voluntary participation.

2. Separation of collective bargaining from QWL.

3. Full equality between union and management.

4. The goal of a better working life for all—not just higher productivity for the company.

Watts ended his statement on QWL with a comment that is identical to the views articulated by the leaders of the IAM—a union at the other end of the continuum of support for current forms of worker participation:

There has to be a greater acceptance of unions. The business community cannot ask for cooperation on the one hand, and conduct anti-union warfare with the other.

Several internal union documents further spell out the CWA's short range, intermediate, and long range strategies for worker participation.[13] Key excerpts from a report prepared by the CWA research staff are reproduced below, since they illustrate one union's views of how worker participation might be linked to its broader representational strategies and activities.

> CWA entered into the Quality of Work Life process with AT&T last year for one immediate reason: to help reduce job pressures among our membership. . . . The Union recognized that this problem could not be dealt with effectively by collective bargaining alone; the cooperative QWL strategy was an attempt to approach it in a new way.
>
> At the same time, the QWL effort can be seen in a broader context as just one of a number of routes by which the Union has tried to increase its role in managerial planning. As the pace of change quickens, we have found too often that once the Company has made a decision it is too late to respond effectively. Increasingly it appears that we need to be in on the ground floor if we are to have a real effect.

Strategy: The Short Range

> Between now [December, 1981] and the 1983 contract [negotiations] the strategy goal should be to establish "model" workforce teams to explore the potential of the QWL process. . . .

The Middle Range

> The second phase of QWL development—perhaps the two contracts after 1983—will present two major strategic issues. The first is consolidating QWL as a part of normal management and Union operating style. The second is tying

QWL into the larger attempt to expand the Union's role in managerial planning. . . .

The Long Range

In the long run the strategic goal should be to develop the Union as the representative of workers in all phases of management decision-making. . . .

The CWA recognizes that the QWL efforts may evolve in a variety of different ways and will be shaped by forces that are only partially within the control of the union. This union has, however, gone farther than any other in attempting to chart a strategy for shaping this evolution and making worker participation an integral part of its strategy for representing current and future members.

Summary

On one key issue there is unanimity within the American labor movement—the need for employers to accept the legitimacy of unions at the American workplace in order for QWL or other forms of worker participation to survive over time. What differs, as the statements contained in this chapter demonstrate, are views on the extent to which unions should take the offensive by cooperating with employers who do accept the basic right of unions to exist in current and future workplaces. National union leaders differ as to whether unions should take a defensive posture while waiting for a more general acceptance of unions by employers and within the larger political and social community before endorsing workplace participation efforts.

Beyond this basic point, the remaining differences described in this chapter come down to the questions of how high a priority current worker participation efforts should be given on the agenda of the American labor movement and how much top level union leaders should assert the lead in endorsing and promoting the concept of worker participation. Ultimately, the strategic question comes down to whether it is better for the labor movement to be viewed as a cautious and skeptical watchdog or limited participant in employer-initiated participation efforts, or whether it would be better for the movement to be viewed as an equal partner with management, and even the initiator and driving force for worker participation. Unions must decide whether worker participation can enhance the effectiveness of their representational role at the workplace and eventually be used as a means of enhancing industrial democracy within American society. In our final chapter, we will attempt to spell out in more detail some of the consequences of these different strategies for the American labor movement.

NOTES

1. The following summary and excerpt are taken from Thomas R. Donahue, "Labor Looks at Quality of Worklife Programs," an address to the Labor Relations Research Center, University of Massachusetts at Amherst, January 7, 1982.

2. William Winpisinger, "Job Enrichment: A Union View," *Monthly Labor Review* 96 (April 1973), pp. 54-56.

3. Letter from William Winpisinger to IAM Local Lodges, April 16, 1982.

4. Personal interview, April 7, 1983.

5. "A Workers' Technology Bill of Rights" in *Let's Rebuild America,* International Association of Machinists, 1983, Appendix B.

6. William Winpisinger, "Who it Takes to Tango," *New York Times,* op/ed page, November 15, 1981.

7. Letter of Understanding appended to the 1973 General Motors-UAW national agreement quoted from Irving H. Siegel and Edgar Weinberg, *Labor-Management Cooperation* (Kalamazoo, MI: W.E. Upjohn Institute for Employment Research, 1982), pp. 272-273.

8. Speech by Irving Bluestone to a labor and management group at the Cadillac Engine Plant in Livonia, Michigan, 1982.

9. For a description of Sam Camens' views on the role of worker participation in the steel industry, see his statement to the U.S. House of Representatives Subcommittee on Oversight and Investigations, April 23, 1982.

10. Personal interview with Sam Camens, January 12, 1982.

11. Personal interview with Lynn Williams, January 13, 1982.

12. Glenn E. Watts, "Quality of Work Life," speech delivered to a National Labor-Management Conference, Washington, DC, September 9, 1982. Excerpts reproduced here are taken from *Perspective* (Fort Washington, PA. Labor Relations Press, 1982), pp. 1-128 and 1-129.

13. The excerpts quoted in the text are from Ronnie J. Straw, Charles C. Heckscher, and Lisa Williamson, "Quality of Work Life: Strategy for Development," Internal Report of the Research Department of the CWA, December 8, 1981. Material from this report can also be found in chapter 6 of "QWL and Participation in Decision Making," a report of the CWA Bargaining Council for 1983 negotiations.

Chapter 7

Conclusions and Implications

The data presented in the preceding chapters suggest there is strong potential for worker participation processes as judged by the degree of interest union members expressed in gaining greater say over decisions affecting their jobs. However, only some of these processes were successful in achieving significant improvements in worker influence and in union member evaluation of their local union performance. Those that were most successful were ones in which the union served as a full joint partner in the process, actual changes were made in the organization of work which enhanced employment security and improved the economic performance of the firm, and union leaders were able to link their support of QWL to their larger collective bargaining and representational strategies.

Union involvement in worker participation has led to important positive effects for union leaders and their organizations. Specifically, local leaders report that their relations with management representatives and supervisors have improved. Training union activists to serve as QWL facilitators has produced new leadership skills and enhanced problem-solving without jeopardizing the grievance process. On the other hand, there is no evidence that worker participation processes increased membership attachment to unions or involvement in local union affairs. The case studies demonstrated that worker participation processes tend to go through a natural cycle. Following an initial skepticism on the part of members and many local officers, a period of enthusiasm and support tends to occur among those gaining experience with participation. This is often followed by a plateauing of interest and support within the broader membership of the local union. Whether the process survives this critical testing period depends on the ability of the employer to achieve tangible improvements in economic performance and the ability of the union to link its support for worker participation to its broader bargaining objectives in representing the bread and butter interests and needs of its members.

Thus, the central implication of this research is that for worker participation processes to survive the economic and political obstacles they encounter over time, each party must see these processes as contributing to their separate economic and organizational interests. While improvements in the psychological rewards workers derive from their jobs are necessary conditions for success, psychological rewards alone do not appear to be sufficient to maintain the commitment of management, the union and its leaders, or rank and file workers.

Implications for the Labor Movement

These conclusions imply that rather than adopting a uniform position for or against worker participation on some philosophical ground, union leaders need to think strategically about the conditions that must exist for worker participation to be in the interests of their members and the steps needed to link these processes to the union's broader strategies for improving the effectiveness of its bargaining relationship.

Issues Facing Local Union Leaders

The ultimate choice of whether or not to actively support the development of a worker participation process in a specific plant, office, or worksite can best be made by local union leaders based on a consideration of the need for change in their bargaining relationship and the viability of some form of worker participation as a partial solution to their problems. At least three conditions are necessary to make union support viable: the employer must accept the legitimacy of the union, top management must be deeply committed to supporting the process and there must be a viable economic future for the plant.

Management Acceptance of Unions. Clearly, if union leaders believe the employer is intent on using the participation process to undermine the support for the union, if clear evidence exists of the employer's unwillingness to accept the legitimacy of the union, then it makes little sense for the union to cooperate with a worker participation process. To support or endorse a participation process under these circumstances would be tantamount to the local union participating in its own slow demise. The more difficult case, however, is one where *local management* accepts the legitimacy of the union in *its* plant, but higher corporate management uses union avoidance strategies to keep unions out of other new or existing sites. Local union opposition to QWL and other participation processes under those circumstances would appear to be a necessary step toward implementing the strategy that is favored by most national union leaders, namely, to force employers to make a choice between (1) acceptance of unions and the potential growth of worker participation and other joint union-management efforts, or (2) continued low trust/high conflict arms-length relationships.

Management Commitment. Without a deep commitment among the key management decisionmakers to supporting a participation process over an extended period of time, neither union commitment nor rank and file enthusiasm for the process can make a worker participation process succeed. This means, among other things, the willingness to allocate resources to support participation efforts and to maintain the commitment of resources through periods of short term economic crisis. Management (and union) commitment is likely to be severely tested at various points during the evolution of the process as inconsistencies arise between other company strategies and objectives and the worker participation process. Thus, the real tests of commitment come when hard decisions and tradeoffs must be made between maintaining support for the process and pursuing other valued objectives.

Economic Viability. Worker participation programs cannot be a panacea in the face of economic problems which lie beyond the control of the local union, the employer, or the workers. In those cases, a worker participation process may simply serve to divert attention for a short period of time from more basic problems and will eventually lead to disenchantment among the rank and file as the problems worsen. Sometimes participation programs can be combined productively with steps such as compensation concessions and other cost reduction strategies. But, unless the economic foundation upon which the worker participation process will rest is itself viable, the union's efforts might better be put to other uses.

Linkages to Collective Bargaining. Where the conditions necessary for a potentially viable worker participation process exist, local union leaders need to consider how this process will fit into their overall bargaining and representational strategies. For unions and their members to benefit from the process, union leaders must do more than react to the employer's or the consultant's vision or expectations for worker participation. As the case studies clearly pointed out, over time a total separation of worker participation from collective bargaining is neither possible nor desirable. Thus, union leaders need to anticipate how the process will evolve and to consider what part they want it to play in their collective bargaining relationship and in the union's role in the workplace.

One of the biggest challenges to the traditional role of the union that a successful participation process will produce is increased variability in practices and conditions within the bargaining unit. Three different sources of variation will arise that will require union leadership attention.

First, because worker participation processes diffuse slowly through an organization, for an extended period of time there will be a group of "participants" and a group of "nonparticipants." Even after the process is widely diffused, there are likely to be some individuals who prefer to not get involved in group activities and problemsolving processes. The existence of these two groups provides a fertile ground for rumors, competition, and internal political conflicts within the union. Since participants are likely to be introducing changes in traditional work practices, nonparticipants may rationalize their noninvolvement by voicing skepticism toward the QWL process.

Second, introducing changes in work practices based on the ideas generated in the worker participation process has a general decentralizing effect on the collective bargaining relationship. Proposals to modify established customs and practices, if not formal collective bargaining agreement provisions, are likely to arise. This has the effect of reducing the "common rule" strategy that American unions have used to limit competition and standardize conditions among individuals and groups in their bargaining units. The standardization of practices and rules established through the collective bargaining agreement and enforced through the contract administration process historically has served as a basic source of worker security and internal union control.

Third, over time there is likely to be a shift away from detailed job and contractual rules through work reorganization experiments which broaden out job responsibilities. In the more advanced cases, such as work team arrangements, the concept of an individual job description or assignment is replaced with a set of tasks that lie within the general responsibility of the group. The movement toward work teams, payment for knowledge compensation systems, job rotation, and semi-autonomous work groups all require workers and their local unions to partially abandon their historic strategies for maximizing job control through enforcement of detailed rules governing specific, narrowly defined jobs. In return, the workers receive greater training in a variety of job responsibilities and more control over how the group organizes itself.

In team systems, workers and their union representatives often also gain more information about the work and its contribution to the overall production process and the economic performance of the enterprise. In short, all of these changes reduce the reliance on strict rules governing individual worker job rights and responsibilities and increase the variations in practices and flexibility in the use of human resources. The shift away from standardized and tightly detailed jobs also increases the variability across and within workplaces. Managing this variability and flexibility without increasing divisiveness and competition will become a major new role for the national and local union.

Although our findings stress the need to link worker participation processes to the larger collective bargaining efforts on a strategic level, this does not imply that there necessarily need be a total integration or merger of the participation process with the *procedures* for resolving grievances and negotiating collective bargaining agreements. Issues of contract interpretation or alleged violations of individual worker rights best suited to resolution through the established grievance procedure will continue to occur. Likewise, basic differences in economic interests which will require hard bargaining at periodic intervals will continue to exist between workers and their employers. The key challenge to union leaders and management representatives is to manage these "mixed-motive" relationships such that cooperative problemsolving efforts can comfortably coexist with hard bargaining and the formal adjudication of disputes.

Strategies for National Unions

Even though worker participation processes are carried out through local unions, the case studies of the UAW and the USW experiences reported in chapter 3 suggest that national union leaders and staff play key roles in implementing a coherent union strategy on worker participation. First, national union leaders must clearly communicate their views on the conditions under which they believe participation processes are viable and the conditions under which they would advise against union endorsement and involvement. Second, where locals are involved in these processes national leaders need to provide the training and leadership development services required to integrate QWL and related processes with broader national union strategies. One of the most positive byproducts of QWL experiments is the emergence of a talented group of new local labor leaders wo have been trained in group dynamics, problemsolving, and team building. Through their roles as QWL facilitators these local union representatives are also gaining a greater exposure to and serving a much wider cross section of union members than most shop stewards or grievance committee members. These individuals represent a rich pool of potential future union leaders.

Along with these facilitators stand the elected local leaders who have taken the political risks associated with supporting a QWL process. Together, these elected leaders and QWL facilitators represent a highly committed group that believes deeply in both the need for strong unions and in the value of worker participation. One of the most important contributions that a national union can make toward strengthening the role of worker participation within the union and diffusing the process to a wider spectrum of union members is to reinforce, support, and draw on the talents and experiences of these individuals. Failure to provide career opportunities within their unions for these local activists entails the risk of losing many of them to management positions or underutilizing them if they fade back into a less active rank and file status. Taking advantage of their training and experience by, for example, using them in educational and training conferences, not only will help others to learn from their experiences but also will provide the support and reinforcement needed to encourage them to continue to be active in their union.

The Role of the AFL-CIO

While there is no expectation that the AFL-CIO, or any unit at the Federation level, will or should deviate from the approach of leaving policies regarding worker participation to their constituent unions, there are several critical functions for leaders at this level that are consistent with their role in the structure of the American labor movement. These functions are to: (1) foster dialogue on this issue among national union leaders and with representatives of business and government; (2) convey to the larger public the labor movement's strategies for relating worker participation to collective bargaining and broader national economic and labor policies; and (3) encourage experimentation with worker participation efforts that operate under appropriate conditions.

There clearly will remain a range of views about the viability of worker participation efforts and their appropriate role within the broader strategies of the labor movement. While it may not be possible or desirable to press for a consensus on these issues across the various national unions and their leaders, it is clear that the issue of how worker participation efforts fit within the larger collective bargaining and public policy agenda of the labor movement needs to be more actively debated at the highest levels of the labor movement. Out of these discussions may emerge a clearer picture of what the labor movement's model for QWL and related processes should be—a limited supplement to collective bargaining or an evolving step toward an American brand of shop floor industrial democracy that is an integral part of the collective bargaining process.

It was noted at the outset of chapter 6 that national labor leaders have an important role in shaping the image of unions in the eyes of workers, employers, and the larger society. If, under appropriate conditions, worker participation is seen as an integral component of the broader strategies for strengthening the roles and effectiveness of unions at the workplace and supplementing collective bargaining, then the task of the top leaders will be to convey this view of QWL or worker participation efforts to all of these audiences. The current message conveyed from the top of the movement is one of "cautious skepticism" and neutrality. One can envision, however, a different message that specifies the conditions that must be present, but then conveys enthusiastic support for experimentation with particular types of worker participation. This shift in the message communicated would again help challenge management for the initiative on worker participation efforts and would serve to further legitimize and encourage the activities that are underway within the various national unions.

Implications for the U.S. Industrial Relations System

Integrating worker participation efforts into the broader bargaining and public policy strategies of the labor movement could potentially lead to a number of important changes for the larger U.S. industrial relations system.

Impact on Job Control Unionism

The most direct effect of expanded worker participation efforts, especially those that involve work reorganization, is a movement away from the detailed job control form of unionism characteristic of U.S. collective bargaining. This does not mean that the collective bargaining agreement will no longer govern the terms and conditions of employment. However, detailed specification of contractual rules may give way to a more flexible and varied form of work organization at the plant level. This implies a major change in the roles of the local union, supervisors, and higher levels of management.

For the union, this requires relinquishing one of its traditional bases of power and security in return for greater information and perhaps influence over a wider array of issues that traditionally have been reserved to management. The traditional principle that "management acts and workers grieve" will have to give way to more joint planning and consultation at the workplace.

For the worker, this new arrangement means exposure to a wider variety of tasks and more advanced training, and, therefore, wider opportunities for skill acquisition and enhancement. On the other hand, it also implies greater responsibility for decisions that would otherwise have been left to a supervisor or higher manager.

For management, this development implies a trade of some traditional prerogatives in return for greater flexibility in human resource management and a reduction in the detailed rules governing job definitions and assignments. In summary, for all the parties, expanded worker participation implies a more proactive form of labor-management relations based around greater joint research and analysis, planning, and consultation.

Effects on Labor Law

Over time, the expansion of new forms of work organization and participation may lead to a breakdown in the legal line of demarcation between "labor" and "management." These changes place the role of the supervisor in an even more nebulous status than before. This, in turn, should call into question provisions in the National Labor Relations Act (NLRA) governing the definitions of "worker" covered under the Act and "supervisor" excluded from the Act. It also challenges the relevance of the NLRA's scope of bargaining doctrines as interpreted by the National Labor Relations Board (NLRB). If work teams and union representatives get more deeply involved in sharing information, consulting, or perhaps even effectively deciding issues that lie outside the issues of wages, hours, and working conditions, the distinction between mandatory and permissive subjects of collective bargaining becomes increasingly blurred and less relevant.

One further potential outgrowth of these participation efforts is development of some form of "works council" arrangement at the plant level. In a sense, a form of this already exists in the joint labor-management steering committees that oversee many of the QWL participation processes.

Linkages to National Labor and Economic Policies

Should worker participation, along with the other changes in industrial relations set in motion by these projects, be viewed as part of a larger national strategy for reforming labor policy and enhancing human capital investment and development? We believe a strong case can be made for treating these processes, forms of work organization, and the labor management relationships which support them as the micro foundation for a new industrial and human resources development policy. It may be desirable for public policy debates over trade or tax policies targeted on particular industries to consider the state of labor-management relations (and joint efforts to improve them) in those industries.

These are questions that the labor movement and others concerned about the future of the U.S. industrial relations system must grapple with in the years ahead. Perhaps the analysis here will stimulate the dialogue needed to move this debate closer to center stage. While the material presented in this book was aimed primarily at the representatives of the labor movement who need to come to grips with the role of worker participation processes, ultimately the choice over the future of these processes is not labor's alone. Instead, the future of worker participation will be shaped by the strategic choices made by leaders of unions, firms, and the government, and in no small part by the workers themselves, as they all attempt to adapt the U.S. industrial relations system to a highly competitive world environment.

POSTSCRIPT
Selected Reactions from Union Leaders

Since this study was conducted in cooperation with representatives from the labor movement, we thought it would be instructive to include as a postscript to the study the reactions to our conclusions of two key union presidents. As the following statements of Glenn Watts and William Winpisinger attest, there continues to be a wide diversity of views of worker participation processes within the American labor movement.

Comments of
Glenn E. Watts
President
Communications Workers of America

This study performs a very valuable function in supplying evidence about an area which has been largely governed by assumption and impression. It happens that we in CWA have recently concluded our own joint study of our QWL process with AT&T; our conclusions are on most points similar to those of this book.

1. We found that in the ten cases we studied, QWL had been successful on most major dimensions. Survey results showed improved job satisfaction, better relations to supervisors, and (unlike the MIT study) a feeling of increased influence and participation among the team members. To a lesser extent, these improvements spilled over to the non-members. Of particular interest to us, furthermore, is that attitudes to the union were very positive, *especially* among those who saw the union leadership as strongly committed to the process.

2. At the same time, we found that many QWL teams run into a "plateau"—the same term used by the MIT researchers—after a year or two. We do not, however, attribute this loss of momentum to direct negative actions by management. In our case it

197

seems to result from the fact that QWL often remains isolated within the organization as a whole: there is a lack of widespread support for its basic values, and higher-level policies often contradict what the teams are trying to achieve. So their scope of activity remains limited, and their view of the future is often pessimistic.

3.   We also found a few areas where commitment from higher levels of management and the union was strong enough that teams were encouraged to deal with matters of work-related *policy*. In these locations teams had gotten past the "plateau" and were proceeding with great confidence and enthusiasm to tackle difficult issues.

These findings support the MIT researchers' emphasis on the importance of extending QWL beyond immediate "environmental" issues. I would certainly visualize QWL teams redesigning jobs; and this would, as Kochan, Katz and Mower point out, lead teams into areas which are covered by the collective bargaining agreement. But I do not believe that there need be any blurring of the *distinction* between collective bargaining and QWL. Our position is very simple: QWL groups cannot bargain or alter the contract. They can, however, make recommendations; if their recommendations involve contractual changes, they must then pass through the normal collective bargaining process before being implemented. This approach, I believe, provides both security and flexibility in dealing with advanced developments of the QWL process.

My final comment is about a topic which the MIT study does not stress. I believe that for QWL to be effective in the long run, it must become not just a worker "program," but a part of values and relationships at all levels. That applies not only to management but also to the *union*: we need to consider whether our own structures and internal relations support participative values. We in CWA have recently taken our commitment to QWL a step further by starting the process within our own staff. We expect that it will lead to the same improvements we are seeking in our effort with AT&T—better working relations and greater organizational effectiveness—so that we can provide that best possible service to our members in this time of rapid change.

Comments of
William W. Winpisinger
President
International Association of Machinists
and Aerospace Workers

The concept of "quality of work life" is not new to the American labor movement. From its very beginnings, American labor has been dedicated to improving the quality of workers' lives. In this effort, joint labor-management committees have played a role but always within the context of collective bargaining.

To their mutual advantage, unions and management have participated as equal partners in national and industry councils, firm and plant councils, apprenticeship and training committees, safety and health committees and local community programs of all kinds, bringing mutual benefits to all concerned. These efforts have augmented the basic collective bargaining relationship's ability to grapple with the continually changing problems of the work place. Workers, through the democratic process of collective bargaining, welcome the opportunity to play a creative role in helping to resolve problems of the work place. They know these problems intimately and can play a major role in resolving them.

To the extent that such committees contribute to worker dignity through pride in their skills and work, to their safety and security on the job, they greatly enhance the traditional work of the union.

In the past few years, however, there has been a spurt of national interest in more formalized Quality of Work Life programs. Corporate America and an army of so-called labor relations consultants have increasingly sought to involve American workers and their unions in QWLs. These QWLs are supposed to increase productivity and improve product quality. At the same time, they are touted as a means of promoting better worker-employer relations and improving workers' job satisfaction by ostensibly giving them a say in work schedules, production processes and the like.

Now, in *theory*, QWL is a concept which any responsible union representative would support, i.e., to maintain and improve both productivity and the quality of the goods or services associated with the company, and thereby, increase the "pie" to be divided through collective bargaining. Only a quality product will stand the test of the market place, insure the company's success and, therefore, secure our members' jobs. Further, if in the process, management utilizes a resource that it has long chosen to overlook—the average worker's ability to help solve shop floor problems—and, thereby, gives the worker more control over the work place, so much the better.

It is, however, how QWLs are *actually* being used which arouses our concern and suspicion. Many anti-union "consultants" and others are promoting QWL schemes, in organized as well as unorganized work places, to manipulate workers through the illusion of being consulted. Through manipulation and rigged committees, workers find themselves subjected to speedups, unsafe working conditions, or divisive peer-group pressures. When improvements made through workers' effort and ingenuity exist solely at the discretion of the employer, they may be taken away arbitrarily or used to deprive the workers of their jobs.

Programs not based on the collective bargaining relationship undermine the basic element of true democratic participation in the determination of working conditions. They are frequently used as an anti-union device to obstruct the right of workers to support, join and organize unions of their choice. A recent newsletter from the notorious union-buster Charles Hughes extolling the "virtues" of Quality Control Circles, does little to allay these fears.

Specifically, QWL programs have the potential for being disruptive and unfair in a number of ways.

First, QWL has often been used by management to divide the worker and his duly elected bargaining representative. Responsible trade unionism has and will continue to recognize management's legitimate concern over quality and productivity. Where there are real problems, we will work with management through the already existing structure of in-plant union representatives, i.e., local lodge officers, shop stewards, etc. Why do we need some new organization when one already exists to handle these matters of mutual concern?

Second, QWLs can be used as an instrument to put the entire responsibility for "increased productivity" and "poor quality" on the back of the workers. With regard to quality, we know from experience that employers generally turn a deaf ear to union and workers' criticism of management mistakes while continually trying to extract every possible minute of working time. Think how many times management has pressured workers to push work out regardless of defects so some supervisor can meet his department's quota. Union members are proud of the quality of their work and are justifiably critical of management pressure to push work out regardless of defects.

Further, no one denies the need for maintaining the high levels of productivity of the American worker. What is forgotten, however, is that the worker is not the sole instrument of productivity increases. Because productivity is most often defined as output per employee-hour, we tend to forget the other determinants of productivity—technology, management skills, capital investment, energy use and capacity utilization. Indeed, most experts predict that the greatest improvements in productivity will come from the new technologies, e.g., robotics, CAD-CAM, FMS, etc.

This is not to say that workers do not play an important role in the productivity equation. They do. Their ability to work "smarter," however, is directly proportionate to the training and skills they acquire, primarily on the job. American industry has always been reluctant to train their employees, unless the associated expense was subsidized by the government. The shortsightedness of this approach is best illustrated by today's critical shortage of skilled workers.

Third, QWL programs, especially Quality Control Circles, often result in significant cost savings for the companies that undertake these programs. These savings result from, among other items, reduced scrap, reduced rework, reduced absenteeism, increased productivity, etc. Does the company get it all or is the gain shared with the employees?

Further, the union must be concerned with what the company is going to do with its share of the savings. Are the savings being reinvested in the operation to improve it further and enhance its profitability and viability? Are these savings potentially going to be returned to the workers via better income and improved benefits? Are the workers who invest their time and energy in the Quality Circle being adequately and properly rewarded for their participation? Or are these savings being invested elsewhere in the corporation in operations which may even be paralleled to those generating the savings? In other words, are the savings generated by QWL truly benefiting the company and harming workers?

Last, it is interesting to note that in Japan, where the current QCC concept first originated, job security is almost always guaranteed in the major industries in which QCCs function. It is both unreasonable and unfair to ask workers to engage in problem-solving to improve the operations of the company unless their own jobs are protected. When American management decides to import another Japanese idea, i.e., lifetime employment, perhaps we will reexamine our position on this subject.

202

In conclusion, management in America often points to QWL, QCC and related programs in Japan and various European nations to demonstrate how productivity can be improved by labor-management cooperation. They fail to note, however, that in such countries both management and government recognize and accept the need for unions in a just society. Corporate America can hardly expect us to cooperate in these efforts while they simultaneously fund and support a so-called union-free environment movement dedicated to our destruction.